CW00546716

About the book

End Peg focuses on twelve important days in the life of a match angler: ten exciting local angling club competitions and two practise sessions. These days on the river bank exemplify the highs and lows, the delights and frustrations and the flashes of comedy that match fishing creates. Set against a backdrop of glorious countryside and riverside wildlife, each chapter demonstrates what draws coarse anglers back to the riverbank time and again, always in anticipation of an absorbing day out.

Fascinating facts emerge in Peter May's match accounts: why the closed season exists, how bleak became essential to the fashion accessory trade, anglers' superstitions and how gudgeon fishing resulted in the cancellation of a wedding. There's even invaluable advice from the father of fishing, Izaak Walton.

For those bewildered by the sight of all those of seemingly sane men, women and children, hunched in all weathers on uncomfortable-looking boxes alongside the waterways of Britain, to anglers already hooked on coarse fishing's web of mystery and intrigue, *End Peg* has something new, something to raise an eyebrow, and something to bring about a smile.

About the author

Peter May has been an angler all his life. He cannot remember a time when he didn't fish, but he can recall many times during his school and working life when he shouldn't have been fishing.

He now regularly competes in angling matches with various clubs, and on the odd occasion he catches a few fish.

When he's not fishing, he writes about horseracing.

First published in Great Britain by Merlin Unwin Books Ltd 2023
Text © Peter May 2023
Illustrations © Merlin Unwin 2023

Merlin Unwin Books Ltd
Palmers House
Ludlow
Shropshire SY8 1DB
UK

The author asserts his moral right to be identified with this work.
ISBN 978 1 913159 67 2
Typeset in 12pt Minion Pro by Joanne Dovey, Merlin Unwin Books
Printed by Bell & Bain Ltd, UK

The author is donating all
his royalties from *End Peg* to
Alzheimer's Research UK

For our fishing books and Peter May's *A Day at the Races*
see www.merlinunwin.co.uk

End Peg

The Highs and Lows
of Match Fishing

PETER MAY

MERLIN UNWIN BOOKS

ACKNOWLEDGEMENTS

I would like to thank every member of the Plough Angling Club who contributed to this book, especially Danny, Steve, Gary, Bill, Andy, Des, Leslie, Mat, Jon, Nick, Gordon, Barry, Stuart, Richard and Chris. Without these stalwart members the club would probably not exist. My apologies if I have left anyone out.

Also, of course, I would like to thank my wife, Sara, for putting up with me for so long, my daughter Rhianna for proofing the text and informing me that I would probably fail a Year 6 English grammar exam (always nice to hear that from a Year 6 Teacher), and my parents for all those times the fridge was full of bait.

The Publishers, Merlin Unwin Books, have been brilliant as always, and I feel privileged that they continue to have faith in my work.

Peter May
June 2023

CONTENTS

PREFACE

When the caption 'Based on actual events' appears in the opening credits of a film, immediately I become more interested. Such a claim suggests that not only will I be entertained, but there's a reasonable chance of gaining some knowledge that can be put to good use in the future, perhaps in the next pub quiz. It's a win-win scenario. More often than not, though, as these words fade from the screen they are replaced by a slightly longer admission: 'Some characters and scenes have been added for dramatic effect'.

My early enthusiasm is now somewhat tempered. After 90 minutes of viewing, will I be able to identify the scenes that depicted actual events from those that were merely the product of the screenwriter's imagination? The character I found most interesting, and the scenes that most captivated my attention, may have been the fictional ones. How can I unpick the reality from the fantasy? And what should I commit to memory for quizzing purposes?

This book is based on actual events. No characters, nor incidents, have been added for dramatic effect. If you read to the end, then you may well think this was a mistake and that the book would have been more interesting had I allowed my imagination to run wild in a few places. But filling the pages with fictional tales of monster carp, huge nets of roach, bream the size of dustbin lids, and escapades that are only found in the more outlandish animated movies, would have defeated the two key aims of the book: to encourage those who have never fished to have a go; and to entice those who already enjoy a few hours fishing to join an angling club and take part in the matches. Falsifying what happens on the bank would have been nothing short of misleading, and would present an unrealistic picture of what budding anglers can expect.

This warts 'n all account details two pleasure fishing sessions and ten matches: the successes and the failures, what I did right, what I should have done better, who won, who lost, who fell in, and most importantly, descriptions of those moments of humour that keep us turning up week after week. There are a couple of admissions I need to make though: while everything recounted happened, the order is not necessarily chronologically correct and the dialogue may not be word for word accurate, which is more to do with my failing memory than trying to be disingenuous. Furthermore, no names have been changed to protect the guilty.

The key to any angling club's success lies with its members. The club I most often fish matches with happens to be full of likeable, good-humoured members against whom it is a pleasure to compete: no one takes himself too seriously; the better anglers are more than willing to advise and assist the rest of us; and all are capable of seeing the funny side of their own failings and mishaps. The result is an atmosphere that makes each and every match an enjoyable event whether we catch fish or not. Although there is money at stake in the competitions we fish, like sportsmen and sportswomen in a thousand different disciplines across the globe, we compete as amateurs. True to that word, and particularly its Latin origins, we fish for the love of the sport and would continue to do so for no potential financial reward. Fortunately, many of the club's members, whom I have come to know well, are happy to be featured in the following pages; more particularly, the type of amusing tomfoolery they get up to on the bank which, I am sure, is replicated in angling clubs the length and breadth of the nation.

Sir Donald Bradman, the greatest batsman ever to strike a leather-clad ball with a piece of shaped willow, was adamant the cricketers should not only read and watch as much of the sport as possible, but also be familiar with its history. It could be argued that the same applies to fishing. Despite the amazing technological advances in recent years, as well as our greater understanding of fish biology and habits, many aspects of catching fish that were true over 300 years ago remain just as true today. Hence, scattered throughout the text are references to the work of Izaak Walton and his contemporary writers. These historical divergences include the methods our angling ancestors used to attract fish, the baits they chose for different species at different times of the year, and their approaches with respect to the fishing tackle that was available at the time. Those unfamiliar with the methods employed in the pre-Victorian era might well be surprised at how closely they compare to the approaches of the 21st century.

Although the ways I attempt to get the better of my competitors in matches are detailed throughout the book,

End Peg is not a *How To* guide to fishing. I am nowhere near good enough to write such a text. So there are no sections covering the best float to use on a deep lake, or an analysis of whether the method feeder is better than the hybrid feeder in clear water. Instead, *End Peg* is more of a *Why You Should* book. By emphasising the enjoyment the sport brings to so many, and how fishing matches can take this to a new level, it is my hope that non-anglers will give angling a try.

Hopefully these pages also show that anglers are not loners, sat on the bank in all weathers, annoyed by the slightest sound, not talking to anyone, and catching very little. If anything, the opposite is often true: anglers quite willingly share their delight of the sport with others, whether their new non-angling acquaintances are interested or not. While they can fish alone, many prefer to fish with like-minded friends, and as for staying as quiet as a church mouse, well this is not an option when fishing most venues and with some of my angling colleagues.

So, if you have never fished before, give it a go, join an angling club, make new friends, immerse yourself in nature, and enjoy the thrill of connecting with creatures you never normally see. You may be surprised at how easily you become captivated by *the gentle art*.

FISHING BASICS

Fishing is the only sporting pursuit that is practised in every country. From New Zealand to Greenland, from Chile to Finland, people fish. Angling truly unites the world in a single endeavour – to catch fish. Given this widespread appeal, it is not surprising that angling can take many forms. More hardy anglers are quite prepared to drill holes through thick sheets of ice to satisfy their need to catch fish; others prefer the delicate art of fly-fishing and aim to place an imitation insect on the surface of the water to attract the attentions of an unwary trout; those with a liking for rolling waves concentrate their efforts on the sea where the number of species that can be caught is innumerable and the largest, hardest-fighting fish can be found.

The focus of this book is *coarse fishing*, specifically catching freshwater fish other than trout or salmon. First coined in the early nineteenth century, the term *coarse* referred to fish that were generally considered less desirable to eat. As this suggests, coarse fishing is purely catch and release.

The following few paragraphs detail the most common methods employed to get the fish from water to dry land and for non-anglers they may be helpful with respect to the sport's terminology.

Using a rod and running line is a popular form of coarse fishing. A lure or some kind of imitation bait can be attached to the end of the line which is then cast across the water and retrieved using the reel. The target for this approach is predator fish, usually pike and perch. Lure fishing is attractive to an ever-increasing number of anglers for two main reasons: it is mobile, the angler fishes many different pegs (bankside locations) along the waterway, and it requires much less tackle than other forms of coarse fishing.

For non-predator fishing, a float can be fixed to the line, some weights attached below it, and then the hook. This combination of tackle is also known as the 'rig'. Float fishing, for many, is the most enjoyable way to catch fish. Watching the bristle of a float can be hypnotic, relaxing, and enthralling. Float fishing allows the angler to search the water more easily, including different depths by adjusting the height the float sits above the hook. The only limitation to this style of fishing is the distance the rig can be cast.

For fish that are out of float range, legering is a viable alternative. The float is replaced with a weight which, due to its extra mass and aerodynamic properties, can be cast much further. The weight lies on the river or lake-bed and the baited hook somewhere near. By keeping the line relatively tight between the rod and the leger weight, bites will show as movements in the tip of the rod. To attract more fish, the weight can be replaced by a feeder. These can be small cages, or other moulded shapes, into or onto which groundbait, or pellets, can be fixed. As they rest in the water, this additional bait will gradually drift away from the feeder and cause any fish in the vicinity to investigate this possible source of food.

On some venues, using a pole is a better alternative to a rod. Poles are tapered sections of carbon fibre that connect together to reach lengths of up to 16 metres. An elastic runs, in most cases, through the top two sections (those nearest the fish) to which the line, with float, weights and hook, are attached. The elastic acts as a shock absorber when a fish is caught. There is no casting involved with pole fishing. Instead the pole is simply pushed out, or shipped out to use the technical terminology, and the rig positioned in the water. To retrieve the bait, or bring a fish to the net, the pole is shipped back, the *top two* sections disconnected from the number three section of the pole, thus allowing the rig to be lifted from the water. To facilitate shipping the pole in and out, pole rollers are used. These stand on adjustable legs and are used to support the pole during this process.

A simplification of a pole is the whip. There is no shipping in and out with the whip. The line connected to the tip is as long as the whip itself, so it can easily be lifted straight to hand. Whips are ideal for catching small fish rapidly, whereas poles are better for more accurately placing the bait and catching larger fish. For newcomers to the sport, whips are an ideal starting point.

Whether an angler is fishing with a rod, pole, or whip the aim is always the same: to enjoy the day.

CHAPTER 1

OPENING DAY

*The magic of June 16th; match practise;
argumentative birds; mental health considerations;
why there's a closed season*

It's 7am. Usually at this time on a weekday I am safely tucked up in a nice warm bed. If challenged, I would claim to be mentally preparing myself for the rigours of the day ahead. In reality I am asleep. That's one of the benefits of working from home. Without having to endure a gruelling, time-wasting commute, I can sleep until quite literally twenty minutes before I am required to start work. A few years ago when I had what my friends and family called *a real job*, spending a couple of hours each day sat in a traffic queue that slowly crawled its way around the outskirts of Oxford was commonplace. Now there is no such trial to face at the beginning of the day, my commute from bedroom to study, a mere twenty feet, can be covered comfortably in less than a minute unless my wife Sara, impedes my progress while preparing for her day in front of the blackboard.

But today is different. Today will not be spent staring at a couple of computer screens trying to decide which word to type next, which horse to have a bet on, or whether I should open that email that claims to be from Her Majesty's Revenue and Customs and proudly announces in the subject line that it relates to a: 'Tax Refund for Mr Peter'. That one appears a little dodgy, though a tax refund would be nice.

Today, as I look from left to right, there's not a computer anywhere to be seen, nor a desk, nor even a heap of books. The panorama that faces me is not man-made, there are no walls, no concrete, and no metal. Instead, in my line of sight is a vast expanse of water framed by greenery. And my focus is not a mouse pointer, video image, or list of numbers; today it is a slim, red bristle no more than a couple of centimetres in length that is slowly being carried downstream by the gentle, yet inexorable, flow of the ancient river Thames. Today is a very different day; today is June 16th.

For every coarse angler, June 16th is a special, if not magical, day. Some may forget their partner's birthday, or even the date of their wedding anniversary, but June 16th is indelibly printed on their memories. This mid-June date, which signals the start of a new coarse fishing season, is to anglers what Christmas Day is to small children. Tales abound of men of varying ages carrying, or pushing, vast quantities of tackle, food, and drink (not all of it alcohol-free) to the river bank on the evening of the 15th. Once in situ they settle down to wait; but they are not waiting for a bite or an indication that a fish may be about to swallow the bait as is usually the case. Instead they wait for the chimes of midnight, whether from a local town clock, a church bell, or more likely nowadays a mobile phone, to grant them permission to make that long-awaited first cast of the season.

Before a planned fishing trip, or a match, I spend a great deal of time idly day-dreaming about how I will approach the task of catching fish and how I hope the day will unfold. Usually this is when I should be working, or when Sara is instructing me regarding the jobs that need attention around the house. My imagination invariably holds sway in these circumstances and it conjures up images of a float sailing a few yards along the river then disappearing beneath the surface. In my thoughts I lift into a fish and the pole elastic begins to stretch; a few seconds later a pristine roach or bream, or occasionally a chub, is in the landing net. Time and time again this image fills my waking thoughts, and with every iteration of the vision the prospects for the day ahead get better. This was the case yesterday while I was mentally previewing today's venture. By the time I had run through the various scenarios a dozen or so times, I had a keepnet full of roach worthy of a photograph on the cover of the *Angling Times*.

Unfortunately, reality does not always match one's imaginings no matter how many times they are repeated. Today, for example, the float did not disappear from view for the first twenty minutes, and when finally it did, the 4-inch roach which had grabbed my hook hardly stretched the elastic. But it was a start, there were fish in front of me (well one at least), and it was time to concentrate and put some more of them into the keepnet.

It's now 8am and the sun is gently warming the right side of my face. According to meteorologists, the temperature is expected to rise to a level that could threaten the record highs of recent years. The sky is a sheet of blue, unmarked except for a single vapour trail from a jet that is transporting holidaymakers to, in all probability, cooler climes. On a day like this, many people would take great pleasure in simply sitting on the bank and watching Nature continue its unrelenting, and hopefully never-ending, effort to improve our environment.

The trio of mallards just upstream that keep flying and landing, flying and landing, squabbling and disagreeing over a matter that is, in the whole scheme of things, probably of minimal importance, would provide a deal of entertainment for anyone with the time to enjoy their antics. Their to-ing and fro-ing is akin to a debate in the House of Commons, just with feathers rather than suits, and with bills of a very different kind. A pair of swans decide to take an interest and glide past me to investigate their lower-ranking feathered brethren. From their body language it is clear the level of contempt with which they hold the much smaller birds. The argumentative mallards scatter at their approach, clearly not wishing to incite their wrath. In every order of life there exists a well-established hierarchy it seems and on the rivers, swans are firmly at the top.

Mid-morning is rapidly approaching and I am catching at a decent rate. This augurs well for the match I'll be fishing here in a few days' time. Constant feeding has helped, with a few grains of hemp catapulted into the swim at each drift through. Come match day I'll bring even more hemp with me than usual. Bleak are becoming a problem though, so I have made a mental note to use a slightly heavier float in the match to try to get the bait past the silvery 'river sprats' before they even know it's in the river.

A little further upstream from the swans, I can see something protruding from the river. In order to protect the downstream towns and cities, this stretch of the Thames is allowed to flood during periods of heavy rainfall, and during the previous winter and spring the region had experienced more than its fair share of precipitation. While designating specific areas as buffer zones is a sensible policy, the vast amount of additional water can cause untold damage to the banks and bankside vegetation. The protrusion is a large willow tree branch that has become wedged firmly into the river bed just a few yards from the bank. It has no doubt been carried downstream some distance before being deposited in a swim that has produced good weights of fish in the past. Smaller branches are easily removed manually, but this one will definitely require heavy machinery to be extracted safely. Or maybe next winter's floods will move it on.

Of more concern is the undercutting of the banks by the fast-moving flood water. Safety is of paramount importance to the Plough Angling Club (PAC) which controls this stretch of the river, so any sections of bank that appear to be in danger of collapsing are omitted in matches, and all club members warned of their hazardous state until they can be repaired on one of the designated 'Work Party' days. All fishing clubs have work parties which are essential if venues are to remain accessible and fishable. However, using the term 'Work Party' to describe these singular days is a little disingenuous. While the 'Work' element is undeniably correct, at such events there's no alcohol, no food, and no hired disco, so they hardly constitute a party by any stretch of the imagination. There is plenty of standing around chatting by the majority of attendees while a small number of members (usually the same ones each year) tackle the tasks that need attention, so in many respects they can be quite enjoyable days, and they are certainly essential for the well-being of every fishery.

While reaching for my flask of coffee I notice a dog-walker approaching me along the Thames Path. Her head is inclined forward in a particular 21st century pose necessary to maintain an unbroken intimate connection to a rectangular block of black plastic. Clearly such a visual stimulant on its own is insufficient because two headphones are providing additional stimulus by keeping her in aural contact with the device. Fortunately the river runs pretty straight through this stretch, otherwise I would have listened attentively for a loud splash in the moments that followed, such was the walker's dedication to her phone. Behind her, some fifty yards downstream her companion is ambling along at his own pace seemingly oblivious to how far his owner is away. He's a type of terrier crossbreed with a scruffy brown coat that suggests many chases through long grass and hedges after birds, rabbits and squirrels.

As the animal draws closer his attention is grabbed by the sight of one of my pole rollers, the one furthest from me. I know what he's thinking; I've seen it before many times. Dogs of all breeds have particular looks, canine expressions that are instantly recognisable and easy to interpret. Eager to prevent him from accomplishing his undoubted aim, I pull the pole back so that it is clear of the roller. As his nose touches the base of one of the roller's legs, I rapidly push the pole back which causes the roller to rattle, spin, and vibrate above his head. The startled terrier quickly changes his mind choosing instead to cock his leg against a tall stinging nettle. Sometimes anglers need eyes in the backs of their heads when fishing the river Thames.

It's lunchtime and I am confident that I've learnt all I can for today. Should I draw this peg in Sunday's match then victory will be all but certain – staying optimistic is crucial in match fishing whether that optimism is well-founded or not.

Although I have not caught that many fish, I have still had an excellent day. This is something that non-anglers often find difficult to appreciate. How can anyone enjoy spending five hours sitting by a river not catching fish? To many, this would be considered a waste of time. It is a reasonable position to take because, to onlookers, fishing can appear boring and pointless. To an angler, though, a day's fishing is never viewed as a waste of time: there is always something new to learn; something to try; and something to ponder for future fishing excursions.

Of course, for thousands of years our ancestors fished for food; to them it was a crucial part of survival. Maybe this need to fish has been passed from generation to generation and the anglers of today have, somewhere deep in their subconscious, an instinct that urges them to fish. Even though we no longer fish for food, in the same way that humans react to colours, with red known to influence psychological functioning, there may exist some inherited impulse that compels us to return to the river's edge and attempt to catch fish.

Whether humans do possess this inherent need to fish, or not, is best left to the psychologists. However, another link to our psyche has been well-established. Angling is of significant benefit to those members of society who suffer from mental health issues in the myriad of forms this most debilitating condition can take, from extreme anxiety to PTSD. Quite why this is the case is as yet unknown; some people cite the proximity to water as the main benefit, others the remoteness from electronic gadgetry. Anglers know that it is due to a combination of factors of which the principal component is seeing and handling the fish. So certain are the findings relating to angling's restorative properties, that The National Health Service now views angling as the ideal therapy for many of its patients. This innovative approach to improving people's lives has meant that charities such as Tackling Minds have seen a dramatic increase in the number of requests for help. Anything that is of benefit to the public, and does not require the use of chemicals, must be seen as a positive for society in general.

To celebrate my successful morning's work I've decided to eat my sandwiches, bask in the wonderful surroundings for a little longer, then pack my gear away and make for home where I can start to plan for the forthcoming match and decide whether or not to apply for that tax refund.

Fishing rivers for coarse fish is not permitted from 15th March to 15th June. The reason for this disruption to river anglers' lives is the Freshwater Fisheries Act. This is not a recent edict from the Government driven by some modern green initiative. The Freshwater Fisheries Act became law in 1878, the year in which Sheffield United staged the first floodlit football match, the University of London demonstrated a remarkable degree of foresight by admitting women on equal terms with men, and Alexander Graham Bell, in a private audience, demonstrated the potential of his newly-invented telephone to Queen Victoria (whether Her Majesty was amused or not was not recorded). The new Act was designed for an era very different from today, a time before cars, before aeroplanes and even before bite alarms. The Victorian age was one of discovery, invention, almost constant war, and social change. It was also a period of elegance, at least it was amongst the few who could afford it. In terms of fashion, no man would be seen on the street without a hat; for the upper classes this was invariably a top hat. Frock coats remained in vogue, with waistcoats and full length trousers. Neckties formed with a bow knot were in decline, being replaced by the ascot. For fishing and shooting, the usual attire was tweed in all of its various forms. Rough tweeds were favoured, being more hard-wearing, the cloth for which could be purchased for around three shillings per yard. Though tweed is rarely seen on the banks of the river Thames nowadays, across the Atlantic a staple item of clothing for many followers of outdoor pursuits was beginning to make a mark in 1878: copper-riveted blue jeans were increasing in popularity with Levi Strauss in his fifth year of sales.

Coarse fishing was gaining an immense following and was by some margin the most popular sport in terms of participation, an accolade that it maintained for another hundred years. According to the *Fishing Gazette* (April, 1877), the borough of Sheffield, where 'the gentle art is followed by rich and poor alike', provided a base for 180 fishing clubs with a total membership of 80,000 individuals. This rapid expansion in the number of anglers led some to feel that over-fishing could very soon result in a dramatic decline in fish stocks. Of course, at this time fishing was basically a way to supplement food. Individuals would kill the fish they caught then take them home to eat. The more commercially minded anglers fished with large nets and their bounty was sold to traders in the larger British cities. In the fishing press, those who fished for profit were often referred to as poachers.

A need to protect fish during the breeding season was generally accepted by all anglers. Hunting, and the shooting of game birds, was restricted to specific times of the year as dictated by the 1831 Game Act. Angling was clearly behind the curve in this respect and although a recent bill prohibited 'the use of dynamite or other explosives for the purpose of catching or destroying fish in public fisheries' further action was called for.

Essentially the key stumbling blocks to the establishment of a closed season was getting the various angling clubs to agree a set period for the closure; and persuading anglers that a clause banning fishing on Sundays would not be added to the Act. Employers expected their staff to work six days each week, so restricting angling to just Mondays to Saturdays would effectively mean a ban on fishing for the vast majority of anglers. Various meetings were held in the larger conurbations both in the north and south of the country and the issues discussed. At many of these gatherings the prominent manufacturer and Liberal Member of Parliament, Anthony John Mundella, could be seen.

Furious disagreements arose between anglers from different regions about the starting date and length of the closed season. Clubs from the north of England preferred the period of closure to cover the months of March, April and May, whereas those from London wanted it to start a month later and run until the end of June. As with so many political debates, a compromise was sought, this time to split the difference, fix a closed season from mid March to mid

June and to guarantee that fishing on Sundays would not be banned.

Once agreed, the proposal was added to the Freshwater Fisheries Act, championed by Mundella who had in recent years enjoyed great success introducing a bill which restricted the number of hours children were allowed to work and further legislation which gave minors some protection against violence from those who exercised a right of control over them such as family members and employers. In 1878 the Freshwater Fisheries Act became law and it was illegal to fish for coarse fish from 15th March to 15th June.

Although the closed season has been in place for over one hundred years, the same debate which preceded its introduction still rages. Canals and lakes are now exempt from the closure and many river anglers feel this should be extended to all waterways. It is difficult to counter this argument: if fish stocks in other waters are not unduly impacted by anglers fishing twelve months of the year, why should there be a break for rivers? A recent survey undertaken by the Environment Agency suggested that anglers were in favour of bringing rivers into line with canals and lakes, but no further action was taken and the closed season remains.

Arguments for retention are much the same as they were in 1878: giving the fish a break from angling pressure should help to increase the volume of fish to be caught in the future. Whilst that reasoning was valid at a time when angling equated to basically harvesting food from waterways, this is no longer the case. Fishing clubs the length and breadth of the country now demand that all fish are returned unharmed. Nor can the rivers be considered to be under any form of angling pressure given the many fishing alternatives now available. Consequently, it is difficult to justify the continued implementation of a closed season. Possibly it should be left to the discretion of the clubs which do so much to maintain the fisheries. Club officials know the rivers in their care better than anyone and are ideally placed to decide whether a break is required or not.

Of course, abolishing the closed season and allowing rivers to be fished all year round does have one major downside: June 16th will no longer be that magical day in the calendar which anglers prize so highly.

CHAPTER 2

YOU WON'T WIN FROM THAT PEG

First river match of the season; verbal jousting
with the Match Secretary; the importance of the draw;
why roach are universally treasured.

Early morning – again! Fortunately the journey from home to river has passed without issue. For once there were no suicidal deer strolling along the tarmac nor any badgers snuffling along the verge then inexplicably leaping out, requiring other road users to take evasive action. Most surprisingly, this time there was a distinct absence of overly-confident wood pigeons walking the white line along the centre of the A415 certain in the knowledge that drivers will pass them on either side. This main route from Abingdon to Witney is not the ideal setting for complacency, though no one would guess from the behaviour of the local fauna. It is amazing what can happen over a distance of just three miles.

Driving through the gateway that leads to our parking area, then past the row of cars and vans, I can see many familiar faces. Anglers are emptying their vehicles, putting on boots, and just generally having a gossip. All are ready for the first river match of the new season, keen to see if the plans they devised during the closed season bear fruit and result in a glorious success. Parking at the end of the row, I open the door and get out into the fresh morning air. In the mid-distance I can see the Thames creeping slowly and silently towards the bridge that has provided travellers safe passage over the waterway since the mid-1200s. The stone archways of the 'New Bridge', after which this stretch of the Thames is named, are shrouded in a mist giving it an almost mystical quality and turning thoughts to its long and fascinating history. There's no place I'd rather be right now. As I continue to enjoy the peaceful surroundings and wonder who the first people to cross the bridge were, what they were wearing, where they were going, and what they would have been thinking as they took their first footsteps over the new construction, a loud voice shatters the calm.

'Here he is, last minute dot com,' shouts the Match Secretary in my direction.

'What time's the draw then, Danny?' I ask.

'Seven o'clock, you should know that by know, Peter,' he replies in an authoritative tone.

'And what time is it now?'

'Twenty-to.'

'So I'm early then.'

'You're the last to arrive, so in my book that makes you late,' comes the reply.

I've studied predicate logic, so I'm pretty sure I could prove with an assortment of Greek letters and some arrows that there's a flaw in his assertion. But it's far too early to have logical, philosophical, or any other type of prolonged debate, so I just smile, as does Danny. I know he's thinking that he's one-nil up in our ongoing, good-natured banter battle.

The Plough Angling Club's Match Secretary stands a little under six feet tall. Before arthritis took hold, his span from thumb to finger tip was just over eleven inches, useful for a football goalkeeper who played at a pretty decent level in an era when gloves were considered a luxury. The sometimes bushy, but usually well-kempt beard, greyed by time, gives his face a long, angular appearance, which can be accentuated by his choice of hat: Danny has many hats, and is only seen without one when he is in the pub or at home. He is easy to spot when fishing and not just from his headgear: he's the one whose kit is spread over the largest imaginable space, with most of it covered in mud. I've occasionally asked him, somewhat sarcastically, what cleaning agents he employs but his replies are unprintable.

Danny spent the first few years of his life in Nissan hut No. 784. During the 1940s there were more American personnel in his home village of Grove than local residents, and a great many Nissan huts were erected to provide a means of storing their munitions along with the vast array of machinery required for the war effort. After the hostilities ended the Council took control of the huts and, once plywood partitions had been installed to form rooms within them, they were put to use as housing for those on the council house waiting list. Many couples and young parents were grateful recipients.

Danny has lived in the local area all of his life and mostly worked as a toolmaker and machinist. If anyone needs some metal lathed to an exceptionally small degree of tolerance, then the PAC's Match Secretary would be their first choice. In character he is brusque, mischievous, and lacking in patience, except for when he's fishing: Danny will willingly sit for eight hours without a bite then return the very next day for another fishless eight hours. His dedication is undoubted. He does not suffer fools gladly, and although we have fished together, and spent many hours chatting on the phone, he is still not fully appreciative of my somewhat off-beat sense of humour – though he is not alone in that respect. Danny enjoys winding people up, in fact it is one of his major pastimes, along with searching for precious metals, so he's always ready with a cutting, sarcastic, or mildly insulting jibe. Ironically, he is himself one of the easiest people to antagonise in a similar fashion. The simplest way is to state something that is particularly obvious. 'I know that, why are you telling me something I already know' would be the basis of a response delivered in a manner that most people would only use after receiving a notably galling insult.

The amateur metal detectorist is also well-meaning, generous with his time, and helpful to anyone who needs advice or assistance. His work with disabled anglers, organising travel and ensuring they are safe and catching fish, is not something he would feel needs recognition even though it does. It is these characteristics, as well as the time he devotes to the club, that makes him liked and respected by all members. As another angling colleague memorably remarked, 'He's like a hard boiled sweet that everyone likes, hard on the outside but with a soft centre'. On match days, Danny is definitely in charge. He selects the pegs we will fish, collects the pools money, and handles the draw. Most importantly, his decision is final in all respects.

With my kit transferred from car to barrow (much like a conventional wheelbarrow, a fishing barrow allows the easy transfer of vast amounts of fishing tackle from car to bankside), I make my way towards the group of anglers at the far end of the row of vehicles. Danny is there, and as I approach he is still smiling, no doubt recalling his opening repartee salvo of the day.

'Six quid,' he says, now looking earnestly at me.

'You got change for a fifty?' I ask politely.

'You're kidding; where am I going to get change for a fifty?' he growls back, clearly annoyed. A few of the other anglers around me start grinning as they get wise to my intentions. My overly theatrical innocent stare is no doubt tipping them off.

'Well, I thought you'd be able to cater for that, you are the Match Secretary after all. Don't you bring a float with you?'

'You think I carry around that sort of cash? I'm not a cash machine,' he's now in full on annoyed mode. Smiling I hand him six one-pound coins which elicits a few chuckles, and one snarl of irritation. One-all.

The club chairman is standing next to Danny. Like the Match Secretary he is bearded; unlike the Match Secretary he is very softly spoken. Leslie, a chemist all his life, is highly intelligent although he wears his intelligence and learning lightly. His gaze, whether directed towards a float, rod tip, or fellow angler whilst in conversation, suggests an easy tolerance of life and the difficulties it can present. Both kind-hearted and generous, Leslie has guided the club onto a sound footing which should ensure it has a future for many years. His most valuable attribute is his sense of humour and his ability to see the funny side of every situation. In contrast to most anglers, Leslie's kit is always immaculate. According to the consensus of opinion amongst club members it is cleaner now than it was when first purchased, a feature that attracts many humorous, and secretly envious, comments. Though Danny and Leslie are almost opposites in character, as a team, along with the Vice-Chairman Nick, and Jon, the most trustworthy Treasurer any club could wish to have, the club is run with utmost efficiency. I doubt there's a better organised angling club in Oxfordshire.

Mat is also in the group. Younger than most of us, he's by far the best angler in the club and should really be fishing at a much higher level. But he likes the camaraderie, the relaxed nature of our matches, and of course the winning. They are all good anglers, and at the draw I need them to avoid the better pegs if I am going to have a chance. Pegs 5 to 7, or 21 to 25 will be perfect for me, 15 to 20 a disaster. I'd also happily settle for an end peg.

'All right you lot, let's get this draw done.' The Match Secretary once again cordially invites us to randomly select our pegs for the day. Normally he would offer each angler in turn a draw-string bag of tokens and we would select one. But in these covid times we have had to implement a different method. Danny now calls out the name of the each angler and draws the peg for him or her from the bag, or the 'covid pouch' as it was memorably named in an outburst of gallows humour at the start of the pandemic when the seriousness of the virus was not fully appreciated.

From the anglers' faces it would appear that the draw is of little interest. There are no outward signs of nervous anticipation, no anxious glances towards the bag, nor any nail-biting or hopping from one foot to the other, though I suppose that would be a little extreme for a match of this somewhat lowly standing. Each seems calm and relaxed about their fate. A few even seem to be indifferent to the outcome and continue to chat with others. It's all for show though. We all appreciate the importance of this stage of the match, and inwardly we will all get that tingle of expectation as the pegs are drawn. The draw not only determines where we fish, but who we are up against on either side of us, and critically, on some venues, whether we have a chance of winning or not.

Danny draws the first peg. 'Bit of quiet then,' he calls out like a Teacher attempting to organise a class of unruly pupils, 'right, Mat, 23'. There are a few rumbling moans from the other anglers, and one suggests we should all just give him the pools money now and go home. Not a good start. A few more get drawn, now it's my turn:

'Pete, oh hang on I've got two pegs.'

'That's fine, let me know the numbers and I'll choose the one I want,' I chip in.

'No you won't,' comes the stern reply. 'I'll put them back and draw again.' He returns the tokens to the bag, gives it a shake, and then draws one. 'Right, Pete you get 15.' Danny doesn't even try to suppress his delight because it means another of the poorer pegs has been taken and, of course, it is one he won't get himself. 'You won't win from that peg,' he adds. Now who's stating the blindingly obvious.

I return to my car and collect my barrow, overloaded as always with kit I probably won't use. As I make my way across the field to the river I feel a hand on my shoulder. It's Danny.

'What did you put 15 in for?' I ask in mock annoyance.

'Just for you, I know you like fishing it so much.'

'Also, remember covid? Two metres please Daniel!'

'Oh yeah, forgot.' He shrugs his shoulders and continues: 'Anyway I've had a chronic bowel infection this week, so if you see me leaving early you'll know why. You'll have to do the weigh-in, okay?'

'Thanks for that Danny, that's just what I wanted to hear so soon after breakfast, details of your bowel issues.' Taking a couple of steps, I continue 'I'll do the weigh-in for you, Les will help, don't worry about it.' He nods by way of a thank you. ' Anyway, what peg did you get?'

'Oh, seven,' he says with a grin.

'I'm going to do the draw next time, someone's got to stop you getting the best peg every match.' We part and I continue my walk to peg 15.

On the computer at home I have the result of every match fished by the Plough Angling Club since 2006. Peg 15 on this stretch of the Thames has been fished 58 times and has produced just one winner. A rogue tench, never caught before nor since, secured victory for the lucky angler that day. Where the fish came from nobody knew, nor where it has gone. By way of comparison, peg 7 has produced nine wins from just 45 matches, and peg 23 has accounted for eight victories from 64 contests. My chance of winning is slim at best, of making the frame a little better. There are a dozen pegs I would have preferred.

At the peg my downbeat mood is beginning to change. Though I have fished this swim many times in the past it looks better today than it ever has. The Thames is low and slow, just as it was on practise day. To my right I can see a reed bed which is sure to hold a few fish, and directly in front of me a willow tree on the far bank stretches across the river, partly submerged. The branches are no further than thirteen metres away, well within pole fishing distance. My optimism is beginning to rise as I envisage catching several 2lb-plus perch from the reeds, a couple of chub from the willow branches and at least ten pounds of roach from the better-oxygenated, faster water mid way across the river. I'm day-dreaming again, of course, but today really could be the day when peg 15 sets the threshold for the best river weight trophy.

The hour-and-a-quarter setting up time passes in the blink of an eye. I just about manage to get my rigs set up and my bait prepared before Danny blows the whistle at which point my dreams of success are replaced by a dose of reality as I get a whiff of diesel fumes. This is the Thames in June and pleasure-craft are aplenty. Initially, being able to reach the willow tree with comfort was seen as an advantage, but the lack of width across the river funnels all of the boats over the same stretch of water, the area I intend to prime with groundbait to attract roach. And even worse, when two boats cross from opposite directions, meeting in front of me, I can almost reach out and take a cup of tea being offered by the nearest craft's navigator. I make a decision regarding my approach, one that should pay dividends: I will simply ignore the impact of the boats and fish as I intended. This is not the time to lose confidence.

Before the whistle fades from hearing, I use a bait-dropper to put some chopped worms close to the reeds; the pole to pot in four Jaffa-sized balls of groundbait mid-steam; and start catapulting a few maggots to the willow. Plan A is fully in action; there's no Plan B but there might need to be, we'll see.

Two hours into the match, there's a few fish in my net but not as many as I had hoped. I'm beginning to think that I should have started with a feeder to the willow just in case I could have surprised a chub early on. Too late now, but it's something to

remember for the next match. The reeds have produced a few small perch, the biggest around 6oz; the roach line started well but bleak became a problem so for the last thirty minutes I've been feeding it with hemp with a view to switching to seed baits shortly.

'Hello. Excuse me.' A voice from behind makes me jump slightly such is my concentration on the float. I turn to see a young woman carrying a clip board. My immediate thought is that this is not the best time to ask someone to assist with a survey, but I reply with a friendly 'Hi'.

'You are aware of the cross country race?' she asks.

'Um, not really, and I'm not exactly built for running anymore. Pool, snooker and darts maybe, but not running,' I reply, confidently anticipating a burst of uncontrollable laughter from my rather solemn-looking interlocutor.

Much to my amazement, without even a glimmer of a smile, she adds 'No, you misunderstand me, we're not looking for competitors.' Actually I believe you misunderstood me I say to myself. 'There's a race coming right through here very soon.'

'That's okay with me,' I respond in a more serious tone. This is obviously not the time for flippancy.

'They'll need more room, there's over eighty of them' comes the reply while she points to the back pole roller, 'can I move this in a bit?'

'Um, well, I suppose so,' I feel obliged to say while looking at the fifteen plus feet of grassland that lies between the roller and the nearest fence.

'Thank you,' she says and begins shifting the roller half a dozen feet closer to me. Would that really make a difference? I doubt it but I'm not a health and safety expert. Smiling she walks in the direction of the upstream pegs.

The sound of heavy footsteps, panting, and grunting is getting louder. The elite athletes have passed by, but now it's the distinctly slower runners who are making their way along the Thames Path. Some are completely soaked in sweat; others are wheezing like a 40-a-day smoker with bronchitis; a few, rather worryingly, appear as if they are about to suffer some kind of coronary failure; and one has a dog on a lead. 'Who's taking who for a run?' I ask with a grin.

'He pulls me along when it gets tough,' comes the breathless reply. Maybe he should start now because the runner looks like he needs all the help he can get. As for room, well the pole roller really did not need to be moved.

I keep fishing the mid-stream swim, now using hemp on the hook. My degree of success is somewhat limited and not what I had hoped. The final stragglers in the race pass by, and at last I can breathe a little more easily. If any collapse now I won't have to deal with them. Time to try the reeds again and catch a few of those 2lb perch which I remain convinced will be there.

Into the last hour now, the reeds have produced nothing since the runners passed by, not even a single dip of the float. It seems that the vibrations caused by the footsteps have driven the fish away.

Word has just come through that Danny and Mat are catching a 'fish-a-chuck'. Leslie and Bill also have decent nets of roach. Clearly I'm off the pace and need something to happen. Should I switch to bleak snatching? If I did, with about 45 minutes to go, I could maybe put sixty bleak in the net. The ones I've caught so far have been on the small side though, averaging about a third of an ounce a fish. Sixty of them would add twenty ounces to my net, probably not enough to make a difference. I should have switched to bleak earlier – make a note for next time. Where have the chub gone? There must be some in the willow, just a couple of 4-pounders would be perfect, so I reach for the feeder rod.

Finishing the match on the feeder, hoping for chub, produced a small perch and two gudgeon. I like gudgeon, or 'gonks' as they are also known. They are a hard-fighting fish and if they grew to a decent weight anglers all over the country would consider them on a par with carp. But unfortunately they don't. There are times in matches, especially on cold days in the winter, when I'm praying for a gudgeon to come along and swallow my bait, or a ruffe (another one of the mini-species), or anything with fins. But not today – bigger fish were required. When I made my final tactical change, I was hoping it would produce two chub totalling around 8lbs in weight: instead I got three fish for about four ounces. Not the way I hoped the match would end.

At the scales, my 64 fish were not sufficient to get me into the money. Pegs 23 and 7 were first and second as the data suggested they would be; my peg was out of the frame – again.

Loading the car I notice Danny grimacing and walking uneasily back from the river. Clearly his medical condition is causing him some degree of discomfort. Either that or his awkward gait is being dictated by the weight of money he has pocketed for finishing runner-up.

'You alright?' I call out.

'Of course I'm not. It's my stomach, I need to get home.' I sense a weakness in my foe, should I exploit it for purely humorous advantage, or express empathy and provide some assistance? After considering the dilemma for all of a split-second, I make my decision and start with something really obvious.

'You go home along the A415 don't you?'

'Of course I do, how else would I get home without driving miles out of my way?' he responds clearly irritated at my frivolous statement.

'Oh,' I say solemnly, 'you know about the queue I suppose.'

'What queue?'

'It's taking about an hour to get past the roundabout.'

'You what?' he responds getting even more infuriated, 'I'm not sure I have another hour in me.' There's a definite note of panic and exasperation in his voice. I should own up now and tell him he'll be okay and there's no queue. But I can't resist keeping it going for just a little longer, and I nod by way of response, 'You'd better hurry up then.' I can see his concern growing, his eyes are narrowing at the thought of what could become a tortuous drive. He is clearly very unsettled by his current unenviable predicament.

'Come on then, give us a hand,' he shouts back at me as he throws his tackle into the back of his Astra, desperate to save what could become a vital few seconds. I just smile. Two-one.

Of course, I will tell him the road is clear, but not until he starts the engine. He'll be relieved but will not show it: instead he'll respond with a growl and make sure he gets even the next time we meet.

Two chub would have put me in the money in the last river match, but they were an unlikely proposition on such a warm summer's day. In fact no chub other than those which would comfortably fit in the palm of a young child's hand were caught by anyone that day. So I cannot really blame the defeat I suffered on my failure to catch one. Essentially I needed roach, and plenty of them.

When the angling press conducts polls in an attempt to identify Britain's favourite fish, the roach is invariably top, or very near the top. Occasionally the tench will win, and as fashions in angling change, maybe one day it will be the perch. But for many years the roach has dominated. Motives for this remain unclear. The reason which has gained most traction is that the roach is, for most anglers, the first fish they ever caught. There is some merit to this argument, and it might well influence many to choose the roach as their favourite fish. Excluding unidentifiable fry, my first fish was probably a bleak, though I cannot be certain, yet I would still rank the roach as the species I most like to catch.

For many, it's the sheer beauty of the roach that puts it at the top of the list. As John Bailey writes in *50 Fish To Catch Before You Die*: 'they are serene... [with] scales [that] aren't quite blue, or silver, or pearl, but a bewildering mix of all three. The fins are an exquisite shade of red that you won't see on any other living creature.' He is perfectly correct, of course, roach are stunning fish to look at. They are also the archetypal fish. Ask any young child to draw a fish and the result will most probably look more like a roach than any other species. The drawing is unlikely to feature a fish with spines, or barbules, or whiskers, and will in most cases not be slimline as in the pike, bleak or dace. And they will definitely not produce anything that looks like a flatfish. Undoubtedly, the image will be roach-shaped. Somewhere deep in the human consciousness, a schematic of what a fish generally looks like has been stored over the millennia: a silver, relatively deep-bodied creature with a forked tail. Maybe that is partly why roach are so treasured throughout Europe: they most closely resemble our, possibly inherent, understanding of how fish, an erstwhile vital food source, should appear.

Roach are also survivors. Though preyed upon by pike, perch, chub, and the ever increasing population of cormorants that make Britain their home, they remain the angler's friend in the rivers, canals and lakes spread far and wide across the nation from the countryside to the most urbanised of regions. As appears in an essay by W. Senior, *'in the neighbourhood of our large towns the jaded worker for small wages finds healthy and absorbing recreation after the drudgery of the day in his evening attempts upon the roach.'*

Twenty-first century pollution in its various forms threatens their continued existence, but again the roach find a way to endure all but the most contaminated of venues long after less robust fish will have succumbed. For their perseverance alone they deserve to be admired.

With respect to catching roach, Izaak Walton referred to them rather unfairly as the 'water-sheep for his simplicity or foolishness', though he did add that they 'makes the angler capital sport.' Charles Dickens quoting from the *Book of the Roach* is more reverential, asserting that 'Great skill is necessary in their capture, although a notion exists amongst many that it is an easy fish to hook, if not to land'. Both are correct to a certain extent. Small roach can be easy to catch, but they are also very adept at slipping barbless hooks. Specimen roach are rare, especially on natural venues, and they present the angler with a singular challenge.

In the river match I was not after record-breaking fish, just quality roach and by that I mean fish between seven and ten inches in length. To avoid the smaller fish I tried several different methods and baits. Although the baits used to tempt roach on commercial lakes have changed in recent times, those preferred on natural venues have remained the same for the last 150 years. Walton, for instance, suggests paste or gentles in winter; worm or caddis in April; and little white snails for the summer. He adds that flies (such as a mayfly or ant-fly) can also be effective if they are allowed first to sink to the river bed, then are lifted slowly to the surface. According to Walton the roach will follow the fly, then 'gaze on it there, and run at it and take it, lest the fly should fly away from him.'

In his *Dictionary of the Thames*, published in 1883, the approach and bait recommended by Charles Dickens more closely resembles today's tactics. For hook baits he opts for pastes, gentles and red worms which are fished over a groundbait made as follows: 'crumb of bread dipped in warm water then kneaded up with coarse bran or pollard and sunk in the swim in balls squeezed hard with a stone in them.' Replace the stone with gravel and it is very similar to the crumb-based mixes used today.

I tried every method I could think of in the match, including liquidised bread, but none produced the volume of fish I needed. Maybe I was missing out on the most critical ingredients for catching roach according to Izaak Walton: 'a quick eye, and a nimble hand'. That's something to work on before the next match.

CHAPTER 3

WHO SWITCHED THE FISH OFF?

Evening matches; annoyingly
playful damselflies; bream fishing through
the centuries; the smells of success.

It's rapidly approaching three o'clock, and I am making my way a few miles southwards to a small lake controlled by the PAC. I should add it's afternoon not early morning, the Match Secretary has not had a sudden desire to start matches even earlier than normal, though it may well happen one day given his inclination to get to the bank as close to first light as possible. On this occasion we're fishing an evening match, the final leg in a series of three contests that run either side of the summer solstice. The draw is at 3pm and we fish from

4pm until 8pm. Having never been an early bird, for me this is a much more sensible time to attempt to catch fish, though I am the only club member who thinks so.

Turning into a small track that runs alongside a field of maize, I can see the other anglers and their vehicles parked adjacent to the lake. Roughly an acre and a half in size, the Plough Pond as it is known generally provides excellent sport in the summer months. Shaped like the lower part of a human leg and foot, with an island running down the centre (where the shin bone would be in the anatomical analogy), it is a stream-fed natural venue, and is full of fish. Peg 1 is situated at the northerly end of the lake (by the back of the knee) and although the depth is only 18-24 inches it has produced the winning weight in more matches than any other peg. Moving down the lake the depth increases to around 6 feet at the lower left corner (back of the ankle), then deepens further to around 9 feet towards the eastern most extremity (the toes in our analogy). These deeper pegs also benefit from a line of trees on the far bank that is well within pole range. The cover provided gives the anglers drawn in this area the chance of connecting with the bigger fish.

Regular stocking has resulted in the pond holding a wide range of species. Approximately 75 carp remain after many dispiriting otter attacks, with over 60 of these between 10lbs and 20lbs; the bream, of which there are plenty, have been caught at weights up to 6lbs; there are a few small tench and chub; and literally thousands of roach, rudd and perch. Despite this seemingly large volume of fish, the Plough Pond can be, and often is, a challenging venue to fish, especially in matches.

Given the fish profile, targeting the carp would seem to be a viable approach. From experience though, this line of attack seldom produces the desired outcome. For some reason, possibly the number of lines in the lake, in matches the carp simply do not get caught. Very occasionally a single fish may find itself on the bank, but that is a rare occurrence. So today I'll be focussing on two lines, one for the roach and rudd, and the other for bream.

The rudd found in the Plough Pond are a particularly impressive strain. Their fins are an even deeper blood-red than usual, providing a greater contrast with their silver scales and making them even more pleasing to the eye. Of course, to Izaak Walton the rudd was a hybrid. He firmly believed that the fish some anglers referred to as a 'rudd' or 'rud' was a cross between a bream and a roach. We now know that it is a totally different fish, but even as late as the mid-1800s confusion surrounded this issue. Writing in 1845, the angling correspondent of the *Sportsman's Magazine of Life in London and the Country* correctly contended that the rudd is 'a distinct and prolific fish, and not a *mule*', though he adds, referring to hybridisation, that '[it is] a thing which, though common among quadrupeds and birds, is unknown among fishes.' This was, of course, before Charles Darwin had rocked the scientific community with his views on the evolution of species. At that time our understanding of all matters biological and environmental was advancing at a rapid rate, but the pace at which these new and often controversial discoveries were accepted was much more sedate.

In preparation for the match, I have been watching the weather closely today. The light, fluffy-looking cumulus clouds have now been replaced by a more solid formation as the ever-strengthening wind has driven a new weather front across the country. We might even get some rain before the final whistle. Fortunately a phalanx of trees affords the Plough Pond a degree of protection from the wind, so for the pegs that have been chosen for use today, none of us should be too inconvenienced by the prevailing conditions.

It would be nice to be able to say that the evening air was filled with the fragrant scent of mown grass and wild mint, but the lake is situated next to a large pig farm. So you can probably hazard a pretty good guess as to which of the prevailing aromas is currently winning the race to our olfactory receptors.

In the absence of the Match Secretary, I did wonder why it was quieter than usual, the Chairman conducts the draw and gives me peg 9 (in the arch of the foot, using the anatomical description of the lake). It's a good peg, a winning peg. There is one major threat to my chance of success apart from my own shortcomings: Gary is on peg 1.

With the whistle blown and lines fed, I lower my hookbait into the lake approximately 11 metres from the bank. My float immediately disappears and I am connected to a reasonable roach. Encouraging. The moorhen that has been carefully watching her chicks has had enough. She shepherds the two balls of charcoal-coloured wool onto the island. With her young now safely hidden away she can finally relax and focus on feeding. Five minutes later and I have several roach safely stored in the keepnet. It's a great start, but in context not significantly better than any of the other anglers I can see. Catching well early on is nothing new at the Plough Pond, in fact there are very few summer matches in which anyone has a poor start. However, this feeding frenzy tends to stop, often abruptly, after an hour or so. At this point remarks concerning the identity of the person who switched the fish off abound.

Though such an assertion seems to be an exaggeration, it does feel precisely like that. The fish suddenly disappear and bites are then few and far between for the remainder of the contest. This phenomenon is unique to matches, with the lake adopting a very singular persona; during pleasure fishing sessions it never happens.

One club member suggested the PAC acquired an underwater camera and conducted a series of tests in an attempt to gain more insight into what was happening. It was hoped that this would show whether the fish simply backed away or stopped feeding. Although employing such equipment would undoubtedly answer this vexing question it would also remove an element of the mystery about what happens under the surface which is one of the many appealing aspects of fishing, so the suggestion was quickly dismissed. With no camera to assist me today, my main aim has to be to keep the fish feeding right to the final whistle using the more traditional approaches.

With an hour gone, I have noticed a definite slowing in the catch rate of others, but my peg seems to be unaffected. Constant feeding with a few grains of hemp and a few maggots seems to be working, though the fish I am catching are small. I need a bonus fish, a bream, so I give my other line a quick check.

While trying this alternative line, a damselfly of the brightest blue keeps landing on the bristle of my float. The insect's long, slender, needle-like body beneath four wings that are so thin they appear translucent would seem to be virtually weightless. Yet each time it lands, the float steadily sinks, at which point the nymph flies away before getting its feet wet. As the tip of the float re-surfaces, this symbol of purity in many ancient cultures returns to its newly-found perch and the whole process repeats. The damselfly seems to find the 'sink the float' game amusing – I can't say that I do.

I should have stayed on the roach and rudd; the bream line is utterly devoid of fish. Maybe I tried it too early? Maybe the bream have come and gone? I don't know, but I'll try again later.

These evening matches are short affairs, just four hours in duration, and with half an hour to go I am, rather surprisingly, still catching. Perhaps my drip feeding approach is making a difference today; more likely it's just good fortune. Whether it will work again next time is unknown; the Plough Pond is nothing if not enigmatic. My main problem is that I am catching very small fish. This means I have to catch quickly in order to build a decent weight. Today that is proving to be particularly difficult. Even with a very light elastic, the fish are struggling to put it under any tension, so given the long ship back they have plenty of opportunity to slip the barbless hook. A micro-barbed hook would help but under the current match rules these are not permitted. In the time that remains, I'll have to take care to ship the pole back more smoothly and hope to bounce off as few fish as possible.

There's not long to go now. A few minutes ago I lost a decent rudd at the net, and the playful damselfly returned; fortunately it didn't stay long this time. Jon, to my left, has not had a bite for almost an hour, and the other anglers that I can see are only catching sporadically. I am certainly 'winning' this end of the lake, but I've had nothing on the bream line and have just heard that an out of sight Gary is catching well.

With no bream landed by any of us, I decided to focus on the roach line for the last thirty minutes of the match and had a strong finish. In fact the whistle came as a disappointment because I had been enjoying catching the fish, despite their lack of size. There's no denying that I have done well today, but have Gary's fortunes been as good as mine? With the scales out of the bag and on their way to peg 1 I'll know shortly.

After weighing-in Jon's catch it's my turn. 'You've Gary to beat,' Leslie says, lifting the weigh sling onto the scales, 'and...' he adds while intensely staring at the dial, 'you...' he pauses to recheck. Come on Leslie, get a move on, I say to myself. 'You...haven't quite done it.' How deflating is that? I fished well and don't think I could have caught more. A bonus fish would have made the difference, but the bream were either not feeding or not in front of me today. Had I known that at the start I would not have wasted so much time trying to catch them. Isn't hindsight a wonderful thing?

It's always disappointing to lose, though I should be used to it by now. Normally we get around fourteen anglers per match, so the chances of winning are about 7% for an average angler, higher for those more talented. This means we all lose a lot more matches than we win, something we have to get used to. At least I get a section win and small payout to cover my costs. Most importantly, like all of the PAC members who turned up today, I really enjoyed the evening.

Angling clubs are well known for the variety and number of different rules they oblige their members to follow. Some have rules relating to minimum and maximum hook sizes, line strength, distance from the top of the float to the pole tip, size of landing nets, and types of permitted feeders. Those fisheries which sell their own pellets naturally impose limits on bait use, most usually that only pellets purchased at the fishery shop are allowed. The reason for this being obvious. The PAC does its best to keep the number of rules to a minimum, but it does have a few strange ones for matches. For one particular match series, points are allocated to each angler with 25 to the winner, 24 to the runner-up etc, with the trophy presented to the angler with the highest aggregate total after dropping the two lowest scores. In the Canal Cup the points system is reversed: the winner of each match gets one point, the runner-up two and so on. The Canal Cup winner is the angler with the lowest total. For the evening series, for which the *Jon Blackwell Twilight Trophy* is presented (Jon Blackwell being the current Treasurer and the person who donated the cup), the winner is determined by the total weight caught over the three matches. Well almost; the weight in the third leg is doubled. The aim is to keep all anglers in with a chance of success until the very end of the final match which, with the chance of a big carp counting double, it certainly does.

After much deliberation and no little mathematics, it was determined that I had, just, topped the table even without winning any of the three matches. My weight tonight, once doubled, was enough to put me in front of my nearest rival, Nick, the understandably frustrated Vice Chairman. The winning margin was a mere eight ounces. One more roach in his net tonight, and one fewer in mine would have seen a different result. Fortunately this one went my way.

It was no surprise that Gary won this evening's match. He's a top class angler with a kind of gritty determination that serves him well, especially when a venue is fishing poorly. Along with his son, Mat, he dominates the PAC matches. Gary is also one of the few members who is not a local, at least he was not born in Oxfordshire. He spent his early years in London. Although that's only 50-60 miles away as the heron flies, it's a world away when it comes to the societal factors that govern the way we live. After moving to north Swindon aged twelve, Gary quickly found out how the two locations differ in so many different respects, particularly in communication. Initially, he struggled to understand his new classmates' unique West Country accents, and they, in turn, struggled with his broad cockney. There were also many benefits as a result of the move: for the first time he was able to play football on grass; while in the capital, football matches were played on either the concrete surface of the school playground or the tarmac of the roads near to his home in Fulham. His new school had a grass playing field, which was both surprising and very welcome to the keen sportsman.

Introduced to fishing at a very early age by his Uncle (an employee of the tackle giant *Mitchell)* several years before moving out of London, Gary spent many a glorious summer's day fishing the tidal Thames in the shadow of Battersea Power Station. Although the combination of a densely populated city, a power station, and a polluted river may not appear particularly attractive to many anglers, Gary's abiding memories of these excursions are of good friendships, enjoyable fishing and, most of all, sunny days.

His match fishing skills were honed after he started work. The company for which he worked had its own fishing club, as many did in the 1970s, and Gary was invited to join the team. Matches against other organisations took him all over the country, fishing locations he had only ever read about. Team building is still popular in many workplaces, but few Executives see the benefit of a company fishing club and would rather pay external consultants vast fees to take their staff to assault courses and the like. A few hours fishing in teams is just as beneficial and much more cost effective – it just doesn't appear in any trendy modern-day management texts. The range of fishing experiences these matches provided has certainly made Gary one of the anglers to beat in our contests, something very few of us manage on a regular basis.

Reminiscing about his years in London, Gary has nothing but fond memories. He also has no regrets about moving to rural Wiltshire and then to Oxfordshire. There is one thing he does miss though. Next to his junior school in south-west London stood a unique shop, one that would not be found outside the confines of the capital. Inside, there was counter, a till, and rows of aquarium tanks. But these tanks did not hold the usual aquarium fish such as guppies, tetras or even small carp. They were home to eels of various sizes that would swim round and round eyeing anyone who entered the premises with such a ferocious stare that small children were best advised to stay outside for fear that their visit, no matter how short, would later manifest itself as a nightmare.

Those customers, not of a faint heart and who were willing to face the evil eye of the eel, had the opportunity to select any specimen they liked the look of. The eel of their choosing would then be removed to the back room and *prepared*. (Preparation basically entailed boiling, very few additives were required. The eels produce their own jelly which acts as a preservative and means they can be stored in a cold pantry for a day or two.) At some prearranged time, the customer would return to the shop to collect the eel which would then be in jellied form and in small pots. To many, especially residents of the East End, jellied eels became a staple foodstuff with shops such as Tubby Isaac's on the corner of Goulston Street supplying the local community with their favourite dish for the bulk of the twentieth century. Much to his disappointment, since moving westwards, Gary has no longer been able to enjoy these freshly prepared delicacies, though that does come as a relief to his family who do not appreciate the sight of a refrigerator filled with pots of eels gently marinating in their own jelly.

The bronze bream in the Plough Pond can be somewhat mercurial, a trait that was perfectly demonstrated in the evening match. While they are caught quite regularly in matches, it is impossible to be certain in which pegs they will appear. Rarely are they landed by several anglers in a single session; when they do decide to feed in a match they tend to be caught from just one peg.

A survey of angling expertise would suggest that the deeper pegs are where the bream will be found, and occasionally they are. More often than not, though, it's the pegs either side of the island which produce the best weights of bream in matches and these are far from the deepest. Even more unexpectedly, the biggest bream so far recorded by the club was taken from peg 1, the shallowest swim on the lake. Essentially the bream can appear anywhere or sometimes nowhere, depending on their mood on the day. While this serves to increase the level of uncertainty in anglers' minds at the start of a match, and no small degree of consternation at times, it also makes the venue a far more interesting place to fish for all concerned.

As a species, bronze bream have significantly increased in size during the last century as evidenced by the British Coarse Fish Records. Back in the 1930s the largest bream ever officially recorded weighed just under 13lbs; the current record stands at well over 20lbs. By way of comparison, the roach record has increased by less than 1lb in the same time frame. Maybe roach, and many other species, are as big as they will ever get, which would explain the slow increase in the record figure. Bream clearly have more growing ahead of them, and the landing of a fish exceeding 30lbs might not be many years away. As Izaak Walton wrote '[the bream] will grow not only to be very large, but as fat as a hog'. Whilst that might be a slight exaggeration, the more nutritious modern baits and feed have certainly facilitated this tremendous growth rate, and it seems certain that these fish will continue to set new weight records in years to come.

Although their size may have changed dramatically over time, the baits and methods that catch bream today are similar to those employed four hundred years ago. 'Paste made of brown bread and honey' was one of Izaak Walton's recommendations; maggots, wasp grubs (hardened in the oven), and red worms stored in moss were others. He also suggested using a 'grasshopper with his legs nipped off', which I admit is something I did not try in the evening match.

Rather like today's specimen hunters, Walton advised pre-baiting on the night before fishing. His chosen groundbait consisted of sweet 'gross-ground barley malt' which has been boiled, strained, and allowed to cool. As far back as the 1600s, when our knowledge of fish habits, including their likes and dislikes, was still very much in its infancy, some anglers already understood that a sweeter groundbait would entice more bream into the swim. While their version of this attractant may have been made very differently from today's shop-bought equivalents, the results were much the same.

In terms of tactics, again Walton used an approach similar to the way we fish for bream in the 21st century. Although we do not tend to use goose or swan quill floats anymore, the way Walton suggested they should be employed is an approach still used today. After attaching the float he directs the angler to 'take a piece of lead, and fasten them to the low ends of your line; ... and let there be about a foot or ten inches between the lead and the hook ... the lead must lie on the ground'. In effect he is advocating the laying-on approach when float fishing which, in his view, allows the worm to 'crawl up and down ... which much enticeth the fish to bite without suspicion.'

I have little doubt that Walton's bait and methods would work on natural venues today. Whilst they may not be as effective on commercials, where the bream are more accustomed to pellets and boilies, following his advice would still put plenty of fish in the net. Walton was clearly a man well ahead of his time where the 'gentle art' of angling was concerned.

Catching bream on a warm summer's evening is a most enjoyable way to pass the time. The bigger fish are on the prowl searching for food, a weakening sun creates a more agreeable air temperature, and despite how blustery the day has been, the wind usually tends to lessen as dusk approaches. There is one drawback though: drying the nets. Arriving home in the afternoon it is easy to dry any nets that have been used; in fact in the summer it takes hardly any time at all before they are ready to go back in the water. But the evening presents a different problem. Leaving a landing net and a couple of keepnets out overnight is a risky proposition. Come the morning, the angler may well find that the local cat population has decided to create much larger holes in the mesh than is desired. In the case of a keepnet, if this is not detected prior to the next match, then the outcome will not be positive.

After an evening match I usually leave my nets in the garage then thoroughly dry them in the garden the following day. This does have one unwanted consequence though: their somewhat less than appealing smell will easily fill an unventilated garage, especially if the nets have held bream during the fishing session. Our garage is connected internally to the house, and holds such vital appliances as the washing machine and freezer, so any undesirable smells are brought to my attention rather quickly by Sara. After thirty-something years of this happening she is at least used to suffering what I amusingly term the 'smell of success', but it did take a considerable time to get her thinking along those more positive lines.

Naturally leaving a wet net in a garage is preferable to leaving one in the back of a hatchback car. I inadvertently did this once while we were staying with my parents in Devon. After a morning's fishing at a local lake, I unloaded the car as usual but with my attention momentarily distracted I closed the boot lid leaving a landing net behind. The day was warm, very sunny in fact, which did not help my cause. I could have got away with it by leaving the windows open for a couple of hours the following morning, but Sara kindly offered to take my mother, her neighbour, and our teenage daughter to a Women's Institute meeting that same evening.

On their return it was brought to my attention, in no uncertain terms, that a net was still residing in the car. Apparently my mother had spent the whole journey, there and back, apologising to her neighbour for the vile smell and in her own words had 'Never been so embarrassed in my life.' To make matters a little worse, she had been distracted throughout the meeting, which apparently included a two-hour talk about collecting thimbles, by the less than appealing thought of the return journey in a vehicle that possessed the ability to both retain and circulate the malodorous aroma to a degree of efficiency not previously believed possible.

My response of 'Did that make the meeting less boring?' was not received well – there are times when I really should just say nothing. Of course, I took the blame and at one point in the prolonged discussion was accused of leaving the net in the car purposely as some kind of practical joke. My father found this accusation most amusing and couldn't stop smiling while he kept rather quiet and just focussed on the televised snooker; I, on the other hand, had to keep a straight face as best I could. My insistence that it was accidental continued to fall on deaf ears for many years even though, on this occasion, I was completely innocent – honestly.

As for the dead trout that found its way into the back of the car belonging to Andy and Ella (my cousin and his wife with whom we spent many enjoyable holidays) during our journey back from a week-long pike fishing in Scotland, well all I am prepared to say about that is 'no comment'.

Not all fishing related smells are bad: a dry net smells wonderful and is the perfect reminder of the enjoyable hours spent preparing for fishing. Boilies can also have an appealing smell. Some smell good enough to eat, but more about that later. At PAC meetings the story is often told of one member and his fondness for boilies. When his wife insists that he accompany her on shopping trips to Swindon (he's a Swindon Town FC supporter and would never even countenance a trip to Oxford even though he lives closer to the University City) he puts a handful of boilies in his coat pocket before leaving home. When the trip begins to drag, and he is getting more than just a little uninterested, he covertly takes a boilie or two from his pocket then, with the same hand, scratches an imaginary itch on the bridge of his nose.

The aromatic scent of the tutti-frutti, strawberry jam, or chocolate and caramel bait immediately transports his thoughts, temporarily at least, away from heavy traffic, crowds, screaming toddlers, overpriced coffee and assessing the suitability of dresses, shoes and handbags, to the calmness of the lakeside and the wonderful sensations that only catching fish, in his case big carp, can engender.

Luckily for him, his long-suffering wife has yet to spot this most ingenious tactic.

CHAPTER 4

A GREAT LEVELLER

*Team Matches; setting the pace from start to
(almost) finish; lucky charms; the magical t-shirt.*

'Fish are jumpin' to quote George Gershwin's *Summertime*,
but whether the cotton is high I have no idea; the maize
in the field through which runs the long, rutted, exhaust
pipe-removing track that links the road to the lake has
definitely reached its maximum height and looks in need
of harvesting. Not that that would be appreciated by the
exceptionally long-eared hare which used the massed ranks
of towering stalks for cover as I approached. But with it only
being early September, the hare has at least another couple of
months before his hideaway is destroyed. The fish in my peg
also have cover in the shape of a small floating island. Each

time they lunge for an unsuspecting insect that has flown too close to the water, they make a circular impression on the mirror-smooth surface of the lake. And there are many such impressions. They are small fish, probably rudd and roach; it would be nice to see the much larger, swirling tail patterns of carp feeding in the shallower margins to my right and left, but I am not complaining. Simply having signs of fish in the peg is a great start; I am beginning to think that today could be a good day.

Every season the PAC fishes a match against a neighbouring club. Like many other top class sporting events, the contest is decided over two legs: home and away. And while there is a trophy for the winning team, like the Ashes it never leaves its place of storage. The reason for this is security: many years ago, while held by the PAC, the cup mysteriously vanished. Quite why anyone would have made the effort to steal it from the Plough Inn no one seems to know; it is certainly not related to the cup's value. Unlike the Jules Rimet trophy that was stolen days before the football World Cup finals in 1966, the PAC did not have the equivalent to Pickles the dog to search for inter-club prize, so a new one had to be purchased. As a result of this minor lapse in security, the opposition no longer trust us to keep this one safe, so if we win it or not, we won't get to raise it aloft in a victory circuit around the lake.

In this season's first leg, fished earlier in the summer, the PAC did not fare too well. In fact, we were well beaten. Home advantage played a crucial role in the defeat, at least that was the claim made by the losing anglers, so with today's match taking place at the Plough Pond a much better showing is anticipated.

Should we lose again today, then it will not be for a lack of effort. These matches, though fished in a cordial atmosphere, are highly competitive. Most of the club's match anglers have been involved in some type of competitive sport all of their lives. Local league football would be the most common, as well as cricket; a few played racquet sports; and many still compete in the various pub leagues in games such as darts, pool, dominoes, cards and Aunt Sally (a traditional sport played throughout Oxfordshire but little known outside of the region). It seems that match fishing often fills the gap which is left when more physically demanding sports can no longer be played to a satisfactory level. The deep-rooted desire to win never fades though.

Although competitive fishing does require a degree of fitness and dexterity, an angler will not fail simply because he is not as quick across a field as he once was, nor because he can no longer move his arm at such a rapid rate. The best anglers are often those with the most experience rather than those with the strongest physique. The reason for this is that coarse angling is more of a cerebral sport than a physical one. Choosing the correct approach and, just as importantly, making the correct decisions of when and how to change a method is more critical than being able to cast a heavy weight further than anyone else.

Commentators and writers will routinely claim that a great deal of a sport is 'played in the mind'. Well this is definitely true of fishing: as in all competitive disciplines, not just sport, the more the participants examine their own performances and learn from those against whom they are competing, the better they will become. Of course, this constant improvement does not dwindle with age. Many of the PAC match anglers have been drawing their pensions for several years (some decades), and yet they are still striving to become better anglers, to catch more fish, and most crucially to beat their younger rivals. On this evidence alone it can be concluded that once the competition bug takes hold it never lets go.

The sun was already well clear of the horizon as I made my way to the lake earlier today. In the distance, the northern aspect of the North Berkshire Downs was resplendent in its early autumn colours, the vibrancy of which was accentuated by the cloudless sky. This glorious weather would be perfect for a day at the beach, but it could play havoc with the fishing, or it could switch the fish into feeding mode. As is always the case with the Plough Pond, accurately predicting what will happen is far from a simple matter.

After parking and unloading, I spotted the Match Secretary coming my way. The ankle issue that prevented him from attending the last match had improved sufficiently to allow him to drive, so he was once again running the match, albeit with the assistance of a medical aid strapped to his leg. According to his version of events, he had stumbled on some uneven ground and aggravated an old Achilles tendon injury, originally sustained on the day he saved two penalties in a cup game some fifty years previously. Though nodding vigorously and agreeing with his every word, secretly we all thought it was a result of a tumble on the way back from the pub. We'll never know for certain. After some time in a hard plaster cast that stretched from toe to knee, he'd been given a soft boot to wear earlier in the week. Today's match is his first fishing outing since the alleged alcohol-free tumble.

In typical Danny fashion, the newly acquired protective appendage was already covered in mud and he had somehow, without knowing, managed to split the back seam. As he walked from angler to angler collecting details and pools money, a long train of what appeared to be cotton wool trailed behind him, snaring every twig, stinging nettle, and dried leaf within reach. Naturally this attracted a great deal of attention as well as a few quips from both teams of anglers. Disappointingly a wisecrack drawing the comparison with Jacob Marley and the heavy metal chain he was forced to drag sadly fell on deaf ears – maybe September is too early for Christmas references.

The draw for team matches is conducted differently from other contests. The Team Captain (Danny for the PAC) divides sixteen cans of beer into two groups of eight. He then writes a peg number on the base of each can. These cans are then placed into a crate, the correct way up, so that the number is not visible. To ensure a fair draw, the pegs are split alternately between the two teams; as a result two anglers from the same club cannot be drawn next to each other. The away Team Captain chooses a crate, and the draw can then commence.

There were only three cans left in our crate as I made my selection. I opted for the middle one and on the base was written number 18. It's a good draw; in fact I will be very disappointed if I do not make the frame from that peg today. Overall, the draw has been kind to the PAC. We have peg 1, although our opponents have peg 19, an end peg, which broadly balances out. More importantly, the visitors' star angler who fishes for Team Drennan, is a regular in the river championship matches, as well as a Winter League competitor, has drawn the worst peg on the lake, peg 7. And another one of their better anglers has peg 10, certainly not a peg I would choose. The number of points we need to make up from the first leg debacle was initially considered insurmountable but after the draw we are in with a chance. Several of the PAC team members looked decidedly more upbeat about our prospects as they started to assemble the vast amount of tackle we all feel is more essential than they did a short while ago. It's definitely game on.

High above the floating island that is anchored in peg 18 to provide additional protection for the smaller fish against predation from cormorants, a Red Kite is circling round and round, his eyes fixed on a point somewhere amongst the foliage some thirty feet below him. It seems to be taking the bird no effort at all to stay aloft; he is using a thermal current of air, his wings that feature every shade from milky tea to dark coffee, are stretched to their maximum width to gain as much elevation as possible. Suddenly he twists his body, folds his wings back, and dives behind the trees that grow on the lake's main island.

Appearing just seconds later, I can see that he has found a small sliver of carrion left behind by the night-time predators. It seems like a small return for such an impressive dive, but no doubt he'll be back later searching for more, and by then, hopefully, I will have filled my net with fish.

As in the evening match, my target will be roach and rudd on one line, and bream on another. I also intend to put in a short line at 8 metres in case I can catch on the whip, as well as feeding some chopped worms to the reeds on my left to attract any perch that are patrolling the margins this morning. It's a plan that has all the options covered and one that surely cannot fail.

As usual the Plough Pond provides us with an encouraging start. Sounds of fish splashing as they are landed and poles being shipped in and out with regular frequency fills the air. The positive murmurings from the other anglers are a sure sign that they are catching fish and enjoying the experience.

We're an hour into the match now and I have been catching steadily from the whistle – just small fish, but I am slowly amassing a reasonable weight. Jon on peg 1 is also catching fish, as well as Nick on peg 16. As a team we're still in this match, and I am beginning to think we can make up the deficit.

Two hours have passed and the volume has definitely been turned down on the sounds of fish splashing and poles being shipped in and out. In fact it feels like a sound-proofing blanket has descended over the lake. It's a quietness induced by concentration. The fish have, as they so often do, switched off and the anglers are desperately trying to find the key to switching them back on. My catch rate has also dropped but I am still catching and by my reckoning I am probably just in front.

Four hours in and little has changed except for the banter between anglers. The stillness has been replaced by the occasional burst of chatter; well, moaning would be a better description. 'Not had a bite for two hours,' I heard the Match Secretary say to his neighbour. 'Nor have I,' came the reply. These remarks are not always strictly accurate and are sometimes used to gain a psychological advantage, but not today. The fish have disappeared from most pegs, even Jon has started to struggle on peg 1. Not so at peg 18 though: by varying the depths I am fishing, I have continued to catch, and with just an hour to go I have definitely put more in my net than those anglers I can see.

A loud splash has just drawn my attention to the angler on peg 19. He now has his landing net under a bream of about 3lbs. That's concerning, I think I still have the edge, but it's much closer now.

'Definitely a carp, a good one.' A different member of the away team is connected to a decent fish which is bad news for me and the PAC in general. Carp are rarely caught in matches, usually about one per season, so it is particularly annoying that this year's fish has been caught by the opposition. Simultaneously there's another kerfuffle to my right and the guy on peg 19 slips another big bream into his net; this one is well over four pounds. From first to third in a matter of seconds; my match is falling apart and, with the away team catching the bigger fish, the chance of the PAC making up the points gap is dwindling rapidly.

Ten minutes to go and I am focussed on catching bream. Just one would do given the number of small fish I have. A bream of around 4lbs would put me back in front, but I am running rapidly out of time.

Five minutes to go and a bream comes to the net – unfortunately it's not my net. The peg 19 angler has a third bream, an even bigger one. I won't be winning today.

At the PAC we still use imperial weights. The main reason is that they sound more impressive: I'd rather claim to have caught 10lbs of roach rather than 4.54kg. Paradoxically, losing by a mere six ounces feels unluckier than losing by the metric equivalent of 170g. At the weigh-in a short while ago, my 101 fish turned the dial to 6lbs 2oz, a weight that put me in third position behind the anglers who caught the bream and carp. On the day the PAC won the match by nine points but still fell four points behind our opponents over the two legs. A good effort by all concerned, but not quite good enough.

As for the best angler on the lake, well he weighed-in less than 2lbs from peg 7. Although undoubtedly trying his best, his failure to land a significant weight of fish perfectly illustrates another facet of the sport, one that makes it even more appealing to many devotees: even the very best anglers cannot win from some pegs. In this regard, the draw is a great leveller. I can now bask in the glory of beating an angler who is far more talented than I will ever be. Naturally this was purely due to the respective pegs we drew, but in years to come that fact will be conveniently forgotten when I retell the story of the Team Match.

In the ensuing post-match discussion the reason for our defeat was quickly established. It didn't concern tactics, bait choice, or even the draw. There was a much simpler reason for our failure: one of our team owned up to the fact that he had not been wearing his lucky fishing socks, something he only became aware of when he was changing into his boots just prior to the draw. From the instant he pulled on the wrong socks, in a darkened bedroom a short while after 5am, our fate as a team was sealed. In fact, in his view, there was little point us turning up.

Compounding matters further, there was my meeting with the hare as I made my way to the lake. According to the nineteenth century Shropshire folklorist, Georgina Jackson, meeting a hare is lucky, but having one run across your line of travel signals fortunes of a very different kind. Unfortunately, the hare did cross my path and, if that wasn't bad enough, the direction was right to left which, apparently, is even worse when it comes to good luck.

Lucky charms and superstitions play a part in sports at all levels. There are top flight footballers who insist on being the last man out of the tunnel, and others who inexplicably hop on to the pitch; some tennis players avoid stepping on the white lines when walking on to the court, but then are quite prepared to trample all over them during a rally; and athletes who simply cannot win unless they have their lucky necklace, ring, shoelaces or the headband they have worn since childhood with them. This is in addition to the plethora of stuffed toys that accompany some sporting stars around the globe.

Amongst coarse anglers there seems to be less reliance on such mystically powerful totems, unlike their trawlermen brethren and commercial sea-fishers who have a range of dos and don'ts that have been passed down over many hundreds of years from generation to generation. Falling foul of any of these will either result in an empty net or sometimes even worse. The PAC's Match Secretary is one club member who definitely has a superstition, though he would not admit it was such. It doesn't involve a lucky maggot box, a charmed item of clothing, or even a rod previously blessed by the Bishop of Winchester while in the shadow of Izaak Walton's resting place in Winchester Cathedral. Danny's superstition is much more prosaic: on the days before a match he refuses point blank to fish the match venue. Quite why this is the case remains a puzzle unsolved, but he stands firm by his decision and will not allow anyone to convince him that it makes no difference. Naturally these irrational beliefs can worm their way into the psyche of any angler. I must admit to also becoming a victim of such baseless convictions in my angling career – twice in fact.

Not long after joining the PAC I started to fish their matches. In the first one, a cold day in December when the river was high and fast, I blanked, as did many others. However, I won the second match I contested. This victory was essentially by default: I was fortunate enough to catch while no one else did. Crucially, after a fishless first three hours of this contest, I ate a pork pie, after which I immediately landed a decent roach. The reason for the capture was then obvious: the pork pie had worked some form of fish-luring magic. From then on I always took a pork pie with me to matches. Unfortunately my initial success could not be emulated, until the day I forgot to take one. At the Plough Pond later that same year I somehow managed to record a second victory without the assistance of the magical pork and pastry foodstuff. The link between pork pie and match success had been broken. While I was initially disappointed that I had lost this sure-fire way to attract fish, it certainly simplified match preparations. Now there are no longer any panic-stricken tours around the local supermarket searching for one of *Melton Mowbray's* finest products on the eve of a match. Instead, I just take a homemade sausage roll – just as tasty and just as lucky.

My other brush with the mystical world of lucky charms happened in the early 1990s and concerned a t-shirt. Whenever I wore this particular article of clothing, a white, round-neck, short-sleeved t-shirt with *Coca Cola* emblazoned across the front in red, I seemed to catch more fish. In contrast to my pork pie obsession, the positive correlation between shirt and catch rate lasted several seasons until one fateful summer's day. I had been regularly fishing for carp in a small lake just outside Abingdon for some weeks. The fish were not big by today's standards, but this was a time when a double-figure carp was a worthy catch, not just a fish that would need around forty others of a similar size to make up a decent match weight. My approach was simple, which probably made catching the fish even more exciting: I used a float rod, lightweight waggler, and sweetcorn for bait which was fished literally under the rod tip.

There was one other key ingredient to my modest success that summer: I found that coloured sweetcorn was the carps' preferred option. Izaak Walton recommended using 'the young brood of wasps or bees, if you dip their heads in blood' for dace and roach, and I thought a similar colouring approach may also work for carp. Naturally, being the twentieth and not the seventeenth century, I did not use real blood, instead I opted for cochineal dye, the dark red food colouring. I would soak the yellow corn in the dye for the duration of the session, as well as adding some to my hemp. It seemed to do the trick. The only problem was that it coloured my hands, and often stained my clothing, but that was a small price to pay if it meant I could catch these often elusive fish.

The lake itself was pretty much just a square-ish hole in the ground, its size varying by the amount of rain and how much water the farmer, on whose land it had been excavated, extracted for irrigation. Some days the lake could be half the size it was at the start of the season, much like a reservoir may vary from month to month, but on an altogether smaller scale. Despite its small size and lack of features, it was an enjoyable venue to fish, set well away from roads and houses. Although, slightly unnervingly, it was claimed that a puma had been seen in the vicinity of the lake on more than one occasion. The fishing was too good to let the chance of a tussle with a wild cat put anyone off.

This particular day I had a dentist's appointment in Abingdon at 11am, so there was plenty of time for a morning session before making my way into town. Wearing my lucky white t-shirt and faded blue jeans, and adopting my usual tactics, I caught well, ending the session at 10:30am with four or five nice carp landed.

After packing away my gear, I thoroughly washed my hands in the lake, but noticed a few drops of the dye on my t-shirt and jeans, the pale colours of which were in stark contrast to the dark red of the colouring. To make matters worse, several of these freshly acquired blotches had been inadvertently smudged, making them even more obvious. Having forgotten to take a spare shirt with me I was faced with a tricky decision: attend the dentist's in what I was wearing, or go home. Unfortunately I made the wrong choice, though I didn't think so to begin with.

As usual a trip to the dentist is never as bad as it promises to be, and after a painless check-up, and not a single reference to my appearance, I booked another appointment and made my way to leave. While reaching for the door handle I noticed another patient approaching from the street, so I opened the door wide and beckoned the rather nervous-looking woman in. She took a step forward then promptly stopped; her eyes surveyed my clothes, noting the dark crimson stains that looked like spilt blood. Her attention then turned to my hands; although they were as clean as I could make them, they remained a definite shade of darkish pink. In an instant, and without a word, she had turned away and was hurrying along Abingdon's main thoroughfare.

Realising what had concerned her I made chase. 'Excuse me,' I called but she did not stop, in fact she quickened her pace. Trying to catch her, I again called out: 'Excuse me, it's not blood, it's just dye.' I started to run after her, but she was not for catching. At times like these it is possible to get a type of tunnel vision: I had only one focus in mind which was to clarify the situation with the distressed prospective patient. Though initially oblivious to my surroundings, as the chase progressed I was beginning to experience a creeping awareness of what was happening outside of my locus of attention and none of it was positive: I had started to gain rather too many disapproving stares from passers-by. They were no doubt concerned to see a man wearing what appeared to be blood-stained clothing and with what looked like blood on his hands chasing a distraught woman through the town. A rather burly, powerfully-built man on the opposite side of the road was clearly intent on crossing and making his way in my direction. Worryingly, he did not look like he wanted to ask for directions to Woolworths. Fortunately the high volume of traffic was keeping him at bay, but that would not last long. There was no option left to me but to cease the chase and retreat, as inconspicuously as possible, back to my car before some well-meaning shopper made a citizen's arrest on the grounds of harassment.

That was the last day I ever fished before a medical examination, or any other type of appointment. Not long after the town centre chase episode, the magic t-shirt seemed to lose its power leaving me with nothing by way of a lucky charm. At least, on that fateful day, I managed to avoid the ignominy of what would have been a decidedly awkward interview with the local constabulary had I been required to explain why I was seen chasing a clearly distressed woman through the town while wearing what appeared to be a poorly designed Hallowe'en costume in midsummer. So maybe the t-shirt was lucky after all.

CHAPTER 5

CALL ME CAPTAIN AHAB

*Trying to improve; the ghosts of fish lost;
the underestimated bleak and its place
in the jewellery trade.*

Things need to change. My match results on the river this season have been dreadful: no match wins; no sections wins; and not a single finish in the frame. Yet I feel like I have fished well, so what's going wrong? Is it just a succession of bad pegs? It's seems like years since I've had even a moderately good draw on the river, and even longer since I drew an end peg. Or is there something else I need to address? It's time for a rethink.

Post-match analyses can be useful and can help sportsmen and sportswomen determine what they did right and what they could have done better. Video evidence, for instance, is especially informative in the more mechanistic sports. Making minor changes to the way a golfer swings the club, a snooker player strikes the ball, or a batsman moves his feet, can markedly impact their standard of play. An examination of replays can bring to light a previously unknown flaw in technique which can then be eliminated by practise.

It's not quite the same in fishing which is both technical and cerebral. While casting accuracy is critical in feeder fishing, and is a skill which is easily corrected by repetition, to improve catch results in the other disciplines of the sport the angler needs to focus predominantly on decision-making. Have I switched methods too early? Did I put in too much groundbait at the start? Should I be more aggressive with loose-feeding? Am I using the correct float and hook? All of these issues need to be addressed during a match, and making the wrong choices could mean catching far fewer fish.

So, a couple of weeks ago I embarked on an intensive course of watching fishing videos each evening in the expectation that scrutinising the methods employed by the best anglers would enable me to more easily recognise my own failings. It was hoped that following this knowledge acquisition phase, I could make modifications in order to improve the way I approach a match. Hopefully, these changes would lead to better results. The videos I chose featured the brilliant Jon Arthur, entertaining Keith Clifton, talented Kayleigh Dowd and former World Champion Clive Branson, amongst others, and crucially were filmed during matches.

Watching top class anglers competing in high level events is extremely informative. The changes they make, and when they make them, are critical to their success. These three are far more successful than I will ever be which makes them the ideal anglers to study. Personally I would not like to be filmed while fishing because it could shatter a whole host of illusions I have about my technique. Far from showing someone smoothly shipping back the pole and deftly lifting a fish to hand before slickly shipping back out all in one seamless movement, the video might well reveal an angler who looks more like someone pulling on a rope in a tug-o-war team.

I've never prepared this thoroughly for an upcoming test since my days at University. Whether it will help is of course unknown, but I do feel much better equipped for my next challenge: the Gifford Fean Trophy. Sara, on the other hand, probably feels ready to move out: I'm not sure she was particularly impressed with a week of back-to-back fishing videos and my feeble attempts to justify the angling-related onslaught. By Thursday she had given up saying 'not him again' and had replaced it with 'I'll get my book' hinting that a gradual degree of acceptance had crept in.

Earlier today I did suggest we could watch the crime drama of her choosing tonight, that is unless she would prefer more fishing of course. I won't push my luck, though, and with the match tomorrow I have plenty to do preparing bait and tackle so I will leave Sara to enjoy a peaceful evening without any of my usual interruptions.

The PAC do not just fish matches on the waters they control. The Gifford Fean Trophy is a good example. Although we are still on the Thames, today's match is a few miles upstream of Newbridge on the stretch known as Rushey, which extends from Rushey weir to Tadpole bridge (one of the oldest of all Thames river crossings). Apart from one large bend, the stretch is almost perfectly straight between these two man-made features, much the same as it is at Newbridge. The Thames Path at Rushey runs along the opposite bank to the one we normally fish, and this means there are no issues with untethered dogs, speeding bicycles, or walkers trying to step over your pole – that never ends without incident. It is a quiet, attractive stretch of the river with plenty of reeds and willows to provide cover for the fish, so it is no surprise that Rushey has been used many times for the Upper Thames Championship.

Despite holding plenty of barbel, chub, and roach, there are days when getting a bite is not as easy as it should be, except from the multitudes of minnows and bleak that always seem to be hungry. Before a match some years ago, an angler told me that he once caught two minnows on a single hook. I expressed amazement, though secretly I thought he was being less than truthful. Later that day when I retrieved my rig I found two of these most annoying fish attached to my size 20 hook; he was telling the truth after all. There are so many minnows competing for food that catching two in one cast is not unusual, though I have yet to catch three at once.

My route to Rushey takes me along the Oxfordshire *Corallian Ridge*, the escarpment formed many millions of years ago that separates the Vale of the White Horse from the Thames Valley. According to geologists, it is this formation that redirected the river through an area of softer Oxford clay and onto the route with which we are familiar today. Turning north, the road descends rapidly; the trees that line either side of the highway are beginning to show the signs of late autumn with their bright greenery of summer gently changing to yellows, golds, and browns. At this time of year there are many thoroughfares criss-crossing the county that provide similarly spectacular scenes of nature adapting to the changing weather patterns. That is one of many reasons I prefer fishing in the autumn.

As autumn slowly transforms into winter, except for the vehicles on the roads, the pace of life in the countryside seems to slow. Birds are less energetic in their manners and song; the insects, found amongst taller flowering riverside plants, that buzz and hum creating nature's own backing track for anglers crouching on the bank desperate to remain unseen by their quarry, seem to be taking things a little easier and causing much less commotion.

Life in general feels far less frenetic. This chimes beautifully with fishing. If some great authority restricted my fishing to a single month of the year, I would undoubtedly choose September, though I would try to negotiate an extension into October if possible. This magical feeling of calmness and serenity lasts until the end of the calendar year. For some unknown reason January just does not have the same character. With the exception of the few birds that remain in Britain for the winter for company, when fishing in January the pervading feeling is that Mother Nature, like the fish, has fallen into a deep slumber. There's less birdsong, the insects have all but disappeared, and the plants have seemingly died. January and February are far from my favourite months.

As I get out of the car I see the usual faces. The anglers are milling around, as they always do before the draw. But today there are not so many.

'You're early.'

'Morning, Danny.'

'Wife kick you out of bed, did she?' he replies grinning.

'No, Daniel, she did not.'

'Well something's wrong for you to be here this early.'

It seems there's always something wrong whether I am early or late, but being early does explain why there are fewer anglers here. Nothing changes, and that extends to the pre-match chatter which invariably concerns the state of the river; the weather; football results; recent fishing trips; and will Danny ever clean his kit. In a way it's quite comforting that little changes from match to match. There are a few moans and groans from time to time, normally about the pegs Danny has included. But these are not serious issues, and I cannot foresee any type of match angling revolution on the horizon. These fortnightly events can be relied upon to bring a little stability and constancy into our lives which, especially in recent years, have become somewhat more tumultuous than normally is the case.

The draw has given me peg 59. What do I know about peg 59? In a word: nothing. Although I have plenty of data about the PAC's two fisheries, I have no information to assist me in matches at Rushey. So until I get there, and can see what features are available to exploit, I am firmly in the dark as to my chances of success.

A major benefit of this stretch of the Thames is that anglers can park their vehicles behind their allocated pegs. This means that we do not have to push a mountain of fishing equipment for twenty minutes or so along a muddy path. Given the demographic profile of our club members, this is no small benefit.

I've decided that peg 59 is a good draw; I may be wrong, the next five hours will tell, but it looks lovely. Downstream, about 11 metres to my right, I have a willow tree overhanging the water – an ideal spot. On the far bank, another tree shades the surface of the water from the ever-strengthening sun – another ideal spot. And although the stream is moving a little faster than I had expected, no doubt due to the recent rain, a 2 gram rig is more than sufficient to present the bait in a way that no fish could possibly ignore. Well, that's the theory, the practice will soon prove my hypothesis to be true or false. With my rigs ready to go, worms chopped, and groundbait remixed, there's time for a quick break with a cup of coffee before the whistle, or air horn as it is today given the unusually lengthy distance between the two end pegs of which Danny has one.

Taking my first sip, my thoughts are taken back to the last time I fished for the Gifford Fean Trophy at Rushey. It was a few years ago, the intervening matches were cancelled due to the global pandemic and extreme flooding. I was on peg 14 that day, and the match was not going to plan. There were very few fish in my net, and those that I had landed were exceptionally small. Late on, though, I struck into something much heavier than I had connected with all day. It seemed to twist in the current, then lay flat. Was it a bream? A big bream maybe? Slowly I started the retrieve, and although it was heavy, there was no other resistance which seemed perplexing. I lowered the landing net and simultaneously caught sight, for the first time, of what I was about to land. It was not a sluggish, disinterested bream, or any other type of fish in fact. I was pushing my landing net towards a large cereal box. No doubt it had been accidentally knocked into the water from a passing boat where it had become saturated, gaining weight with every drop of moisture it absorbed. As I was reaching for the offending item with the landing net, it disappeared; the hook had finally torn through the cardboard and my rig was free. I watched the cardboard container slowly sink out of sight, and out of reach, to lay in wait for another unsuspecting angler's rig.

According to my watch there was only half an hour to go, so I quickly re-baited and recast. Within seconds the float buried beneath the surface and I struck. Again it was heavy.

A milk carton to accompany the cereal box possibly? No, not this time. Finally I had a decent fish on my line: a big chub well over 4lbs. I managed to keep it away from the snags, and soon had it nearing the landing net. Then, just like the cereal box a few minutes before, it disappeared from view. My formally arched rod was straight again, and the line was loose. The fish was lost, and it's fair to say that I was not pleased about it. As I re-baited I noticed the reason the chub had so easily escaped: the hook was almost straight. The weight of the cereal box had weakened the fine wire, possibly even bent it a little out of shape, and the chub had finished the job, turning the once curved hook back into its original straight form. In my haste to get a baited hook back in the water, with only a few minutes of the match remaining, I had not checked it thoroughly. It was a case of 'more haste, less speed' or, more specifically, careless fishing.

Remarkably the catalogue of errors was not to end there. At 2pm I started to pack my gear away. I hadn't heard the whistle, but I was so far away from Danny that I didn't expect to. Something, though, just didn't feel right. There were no anglers walking around, no increase in the chat level. From my peg I could not see any of the others, but I fully expected to hear them. I decided to have a walk myself and strolled up to the next peg where I found Des still fishing.

'Didn't you hear the whistle?' I asked.

'He's not blown it yet has he?'

'Well, it's ten past two.'

'No it's not. It's ten past one,' Des replied with a curious look on his face. 'Did you forget to turn your watch back?' I just stared back in stunned silence; Des netted a small roach, then looked back at me with a smile on his face. I simply shook my head in disbelief.

On the first day of Greenwich Mean Time my watch remained set to British Summer Time, so was an hour ahead. Had I remembered to change it, I would not have been in such as rush to recast and would have changed the hook after the cereal box incident. In which case I would not have lost the chub, and may have won the match. Or so I reasoned.

'Oh well, these things happen,' Sara said when I got home, 'just put it behind you and forget about it.' Good advice though that was, implementing it was not easy. I had dreams, or rather nightmares, haunting my sleep for weeks, months even. When I closed my eyes at night I could feel the chub lunging and twisting in the water, then the instant of anguish as it gracefully swam back freely to its watery lair. I just could not get the image out of my mind so, like a football goalkeeper who has just gifted the opposition an easy goal, I desperately searched for someone else to blame in order to assuage my own feeling of failure. My prime target was the person who had inadvertently dropped the cereal box into the river – if indeed it was inadvertent. Maybe it was not an accident at all; maybe it was done on purpose, in which case I was just the unlucky victim of a litter bug. But surely even the least reverential boater would not intentionally pollute a waterway in such a fashion, would they? A more reasonable assumption was that the fault lay with the hook manufacturer. The wire could have been faulty, or damaged, or just poor quality. That's more likely, I had simply selected a dodgy hook.

Of course, I was just clutching at straws; there was no realistic justification for blaming anyone else. The fault was entirely of my own making. I knew it from the instant it happened, but even so it was still difficult to accept. In an effort to mentally anaesthetise myself to the catastrophe (at least in my mind it was catastrophe), I replayed the event over and over again in the vain hope that greater familiarity would somehow make it feel less significant and ultimately fade from my thoughts altogether. Not surprisingly, this approach, which lacked any kind of rigorous psychological foundation, failed to work. The memory was, and still is, most vivid. If I could 'slay the dragon', that might help. Captain Ahab was haunted by a certain whale, for me it's the Gifford Fean Trophy. To win this trophy, if not today then next year or the year after, might possibly end my torment over the lost chub. It's a long shot, but it might just work.

The peace-shattering wail of the air horn shakes me from my deep thoughts of matches past, and startles me to such an extent that I somehow contrive to release my grip on the now empty coffee cup. After bouncing off my knee, an action that appears to give it both spin and impetus, the receptacle lands softly on the bank where the rotational energy it has gained provides sufficient motivation for it to embark on the short journey to the river. Although rolling painfully slowly I still cannot quite prevent it reaching the water's edge where, much to my relief, it pauses, apparently waiting patiently for collection. I make a final lurch forward trying desperately to avoid the various items of fishing tackle strewn around the peg, but then realise the mug was just toying with me; it has other ideas. With my finger tips just a matter of inches from the rim, the errant cup makes one more defiant turn, just enough to take it into the stream.

When I finally get a hand on the vessel it is not only partially filled with the latest Chateaux Thames vintage, but the previously unblemished outer surface is now a patchwork of mud, and other much less desirable bankside detritus, making it more reminiscent of a painting by an abstract artist obsessed with earth tones. Leslie has probably brought washing up liquid, clean water and a tea cloth with him in case of such emergencies I, on the other hand, have a well-used fishing rag: coffee straight from the flask will be the order of the day from now on.

My selected lines are now fed, and I have decided to start under the tree in the margin to my right. Worm is my chosen bait and my hope is that I will soon be unhooking a big perch. The current is much weaker near the margin, so I allow the float to carry the worm steadily to where I expect the fish to be. Holding the rig back I can get the worm to lift off the river bed then fall gently, and appealingly. Nothing, so I retrieve the rig and start again. This time I'll leave it longer in the 'hot spot'.

As the float nears the outer branch of the willow, my level of anticipation and heart-rate rises; there's got to be a fish there. Give it more time, there's one there. So I'll wait. But the float obstinately is remaining fully visible; I'll give it a little longer. Patience is the key to fishing. The float has just begun to move slowly, and not in motion with the current. It could be a sign of a fish, hopefully not a crayfish. Now it is gently swaying to the left – definitely a fish. The action continues and the tip has started to dip below the surface. Don't strike too early, I tell myself, it's a big worm so give him a couple of seconds.

I can't wait that long, patience has never been my strong suit, so I lift the pole and connect with the fish. Finally something planned for at Rushey seems to be going in my favour. The perch thrashes his head from side to side, and I impart some side strain attempting to get the fish away from the potential tree roots. I manage to get him clear, then he decides otherwise and darts back to the cover. There's a sickening feeling of the snag. Keep the pressure on, he'll move out. He's not moving out, in fact I can feel him diving deeper into the sanctuary of the roots and submerged branches. You've got to get this fish in the net, I mumble under my breath. Though I give myself these 'pep' talks often, they rarely work.

Suddenly a loud crashing sound fills the air. It's one of the many sounds that give a pole angler nightmares, although it is not quite on a par with 'sorry I think I just stood on your pole'. The connector that links the elastic to the line has just smashed into the pole tip. This means one thing: the fight is over, the fish is free, and I am left confounded. How did that happen? On examination, the rig seems to be fine; I can only assume that the hook-hold was weak, a detail expertly exploited by the wily old perch. Why didn't I wait those extra seconds before striking? I am beginning to believe that I have upset the fishing Gods that inhabit the Thames at Rushey.

Regaining my composure and with my heart rate back to a more acceptable level, I have decided to give it another five minutes under the tree and then switch to the roach line down the middle of the river.

Three hours in and it is fair to say that it has not been a 'fish-a-chuck'. A few roach at the start gave me cause for hope, but they soon disappeared. Maggots were the only bait they were interested in, but so too were the bleak. Hemp, tares and elderberries have all been ignored for some inexplicable reason. The waggler line has produced a few chub and dace, but all were exceptionally small, maybe an ounce or just over. The margin is dead.

'Baggin' up?' Mat has strolled up from the next peg to see how I am getting on. That's a good sign; he only ever leaves his seatbox if he's struggling, and if Mat is struggling then everyone is struggling.

'Definitely not,' I reply, 'not had a bite for a good twenty minutes.'

'Same here,' he pauses then adds 'I don't like Rushey.' He doesn't mean it of course, such sentiments are purely a product of frustration.

The float has dipped and I'm into a fish. Small though it is, at least it's a fish. We keep chatting, and I get another, then another. 'You're having me on, I know you, I bet you've got ten pounds of roach in that net.'

'No, honestly, Mat, I've nothing of note, you've brought me some luck.' He's clearly not convinced as he returns to his peg. As soon as he leaves the fish stop feeding. I should call him back I suppose to see if he brings me more good fortune.

Bleak and minnows have been a problem all morning and they also now seem to be working in tandem to cause even more irritation. A short while ago I lowered my rig into the centre of the river and could see a bleak had taken the bait immediately. Shipping the pole back I disconnected the top three kit and lifted the fish to hand. But not quite: on leaving

the water the fish fell off. So I changed the mangled bait, dropped the rig in the margin, reconnected the top three to the number four section and shipped the rig back out. As I placed the float where I have been feeding I noticed the tiniest of minnows hanging off the hook. Lowering the rig, I then had to ship back, disconnect, and lift the fish to hand. Again, not quite: the minnow fell off. If there's anything to make an angler wonder why he's is bothering, then that's pretty close to it. Time for a coffee – but not from the cup.

As I drink my purposely cooled coffee I have an idea. Why fight the bleak? Why not target them instead? By catching the bleak I will be putting weight in my net, albeit a light weight. I will also be reducing the number of these annoying fish that constantly interfere with my attempts to catch the better quality specimens. After thinning them out a little I can return to the roach. It sounds good in my head, but timing will be important. Initially I have decided to bleak snatch for twenty minutes and count the number I catch. If the catch rate is slow I will end the experiment early. So here goes, twenty minutes of bleak snatching and let's hope it works.

Twenty minutes of bleak snatching has put an additional forty fish in the net. None weighed more than half an ounce, so I've possibly increased my total weight by about a pound. In the context of how this peg has fished today that's not too bad; in fact I wish I had tried it earlier. With only forty minutes of the match remaining I have to decide whether to continue on the whip after the bleak, or try for something better. The river is not fishing well today otherwise Mat would not have been along for a chat, but we are fishing over such a wide area that someone surely has a few decent fish, maybe a chub or two. Another forty minutes on the whip might give me an extra two pounds at the most, probably not enough. It's a difficult decision to make, but I think I'll return to the roach.

Just two small roach and a tiny perch is all I have added since switching back in search of better quality. I should have stayed with the bleak. A quick run through with the waggler in search of a rogue chub produced nothing of note and with fifteen minutes to go I am facing another poor match result. I need a big fish, I'd settle for just one, but I need it quickly. My only option is the margin line where I lost the perch earlier. I have previously caught the same perch twice in one session, so maybe he's back searching for more worms.

I've been running the margin rig through the swim for a few minutes without success. My watch suggests that only two minutes remain (this year it's correct). Danny is no doubt rummaging about in his tackle bag looking for the air horn. Did the float twitch then? I'm sure it did. Whether it did or not it is certainly moving now. Give it time.

Finally it's disappeared, after five hours of frustration maybe the river Gods have decided to smile on me. I lift into the fish, and it feels heavy. The air horn screams its familiar tune along the river. 'Fish on!' I shout. The PAC allows an angler an extra ten minutes to land a fish hooked before the match ends. Ten minutes should be plenty, though the fish does feel bigger than the one I lost earlier. He is also fighting very differently, there's no jagged head shaking, or attempts to lunge back to the safety of the tree roots. I now have him under control, he's closer to the centre of the river than the margin, and I can feel a sense of ease has replaced my somewhat stressed demeanour of a few seconds ago. I shouldn't lose him now. But what is he? Bream maybe, or possibly a very lethargic chub? At least I know for certain there's no cereal box involved this time. If I knew what species he was, then I'd have a better idea about how to play him. I'll put more tension on the elastic and try to ease him to the surface.

The additional pressure works and I can feel him steadily coming up through the water course, nearer and nearer the surface. Suddenly he is visible: long and slim, a dorsal fin located near to his tail, an elongated jaw perfectly designed for swallowing small fish, and two dark eyes staring at me. I'm staring back but in total disbelief. He's almost smiling. It's as if he's read the PAC book of match rules and paid particular attention to paragraph 24: 'All fish caught are eligible for weighing, with the exception of game fish, pike, and crustaceans'. What I have been playing so cautiously to ensure I don't miss another chance of winning the match is a pike of about 3lbs that is quite content to be landed and returned to the Thames a few seconds later. The match is over, I lost a good perch, caught a few small fish, and a pike tricked me into thinking I had a match winner on the end of the line. Not the best of days.

'What have you got, load of tiddlers as usual?' is Danny's warm greeting as he arrives with the scales.

'A few small fish, that's all,' is my rather downbeat reply, 'but I did lose a big perch, and caught a pike.'

'You can't count pike or fish you lose, you know that.' Thanks for the expression of commiseration Danny, I thought. 'Get them on the scales then, there's not a lot to beat,' he adds which sounds promising.

After an amount of deliberation and double-checking, Danny is satisfied with the weight. 'You've won this,' he says walking away.

'But what about your fish, you've still to weigh your own net. No doubt it's full.'

'I've got less than a pound, I tried for a chub for the last two hours and didn't get one.'

On a day when everything possible went wrong, I won my first river match of the season – but only just: the winning margin was twelve ounces. My decision to target the bleak paid off. Maybe now the lost chub and cereal box incident will stop haunting my dreams – I can only hope so.

It is fair to say that the bleak is not highly regarded by many anglers. I doubt it would feature on anyone's list of *top ten favourite fish*. There are good reasons for this. The bleak is a small, silvery fish that rarely exceeds three ounces in weight. They offer little by way of a fight, nor are they a difficult fish to tempt. Bleak feed ravenously, a trait that can make them a nuisance to anglers when better quarry is hoped for. Their up-turned mouths are particularly well suited to taking bait from the surface which, combined with a high degree of nimbleness, makes them more adept than most fish at catching flies or anything else that lands on the surface of the river, including maggots. For this reason the bleak was often referred to as the *water swallow*.

In years gone by, bleak were often caught for food. Naturally a great many would have been required to feed a large family, so techniques were developed that put several fish on the bank at once. One method incorporated the use of between six and eight hooks assembled in a *paternoster* style. This could, on occasion, account for as many as five fish at once. After treating the bleak with salt, it was claimed that they made a reasonable freshwater version of the anchovy.

In the nineteenth century, bleak were the first choice bait for catching trout on the Thames with their bright, shiny scales deemed to be perfect for a sink and draw approach. According to catch reports, bleak accounted for many of the largest trout caught during the century. However, it was the similarity of the bleak's scales to *Mother of Pearl* that almost resulted in the extinction of the species in some parts of Europe. The metallic lustre of the scales is produced by a silvery pigment which, once discovered, was in great demand by the makers of decorative imitation pearls and other fashion accessories. The pearl earring worn by Johannes Vermeer's muse who the artist depicted in his most esteemed work, *Girl With A Pearl Earring*, was in all likelihood a glass bead that had been coated in this way.

Unfortunately for the bleak, only four ounces of pigment could be collected from 1lb of scales, and given their diminutive size it took 4,000 fish to provide this weight. With factories capable of producing 10,000 imitation pearl beads per week, it is easy to see how this would have made a considerable dent in the bleak population.

Though harvesting bleak on this scale for cosmetic purposes is, fortunately, no longer considered viable, targeting them in matches remains an option. Without the bleak I would not have won the Gifford Fean Trophy, and numerous match successes by other anglers can be put down to this most prolific of all fish.

As far back as 1877, bleak were the key fish to many a victory. Mr Senneck, fishing with the Sir Hugh Myddleton Club, for example, won a 'case of birds for gross weight of bleak and gudgeon.' More recently some staggering weights of bleak have been landed in contests on the river Wye. One of the most remarkable angling feats was the capture of over

2,000 bleak by Hadrian Whittle in a five-hour contest. The haul produced a total weight of just over 50lbs and equated to roughly seven fish per minute with each bleak weighing a little under half-an-ounce on average. Although bleak are not difficult to catch, and to some are a nuisance which the rivers could do without, achievements such as Whittle's must be admired in terms of the technical skill required to get the fish from the river and into the net at such a pace, as well as the fishing know-how that enabled him to keep the fish feeding and in front of him for the full duration of the match.

A 50lbs carp would be the dream of many anglers, but catching 50lbs of bleak in five hours is arguably an equivalent achievement.

CHAPTER 6

WHERE HAVE ALL THE TREES GONE?

Bankside vegetation; rogue television aerials; tough fishing; the evolution and importance of the River Thames.

At the moment I am in my car, still on the driveway, waiting for the condensation to clear from the screen; it's an early morning in late autumn. The sky is dark and foreboding and the rain is battering the roof of the vehicle like a descent of woodpeckers attempting to emulate a Ginger Baker drum solo. Why aren't I still in bed? Just running from house to car, a distance of no more than ten feet, I managed to get soaked, such is the downpour, so the prospect of sitting by the bank as the rain descends in torrents for the next five hours is not overly attractive.

I said I would fish, a rash promise made before checking the forecast, so I'll fish – regardless of the weather – and I'd better get going. But I need some music. Choice of music is the first major decision of the day. An assortment of Blues maybe? Or something more artiste specific? For my trip to Rushey I played *Cream's Disraeli Gears* album, and I won that match, so I think I will try it again. Not that I am superstitious, of course, it's just a good album.

Driving through the village I notice a shopper scurrying home with his arms filled with a Sunday newspaper. Why is he out in this weather so early? Will he be able to get home before the rain manages to totally disintegrate the paper? Why do they print Sunday papers that take so long to read? And is that why he has to buy them so early? Stop asking yourself stupid questions and focus on the road.

At the river I notice the anglers huddled together under the hedgerow. Their body language is far more animated than usual, which is somewhat strange given the weather. There are few smiles, and that means something's wrong; I think I can guess what it is.

'Have you seen it?' Gary asks the instant I get out of the car. He is clearly upset and annoyed.

'Yes, I saw it earlier in the week.'

'Who did it?'

'Apparently, it was the landowner under instructions from the Environment Agency.'

'But why? Why would they do that?' A pained expression spreads across his face.

'I spoke to the Environment Agency. They told me it was national policy. Apparently the Thames is no longer a river, it's a highway, whatever that means, and space needs to be provided for the boats.' Not surprisingly Gary has a look of incredulity on his face.

I must admit the sight was shocking. The willow trees that lined the northerly bank of the river from peg 15 to peg 26 made for a spectacle of greenery that, given their age, Charles Dickens would have witnessed and approved of while strolling along the riverside making notes for his *Dictionary of the Thames*. These few hundred yards of bank capture the Upper Thames in all its glory. Artists regularly try to replicate this striking display on canvas, and photographers have been seen to lurch from standing to crouching, then to sitting, in order to get the best angle for their images which they hope will soon adorn the walls of the living rooms and hallways up and down the country. Now, this vibrant green, gently swaying panorama of branches and leaves has been replaced by one more fitting the backdrop of a post-apocalyptic science fiction film. The willow trees that stood twenty feet or more in height have been reduced to mere stumps.

'It's a disaster,' Gary continues, 'how much damage will this do to fish stocks?'

It's a good question. The trees not only lined the bank, they extended out into the river creating crucial interruptions to the flow of the water. With this protective barrier in place, the bank was less prone to erosion during the regular floods and provided the animals and birds, particularly the kingfishers, with perfect nesting places. For the fish, the slack water created by these natural obstructions was vital to their survival when the current was too strong or sapped too much energy at times of the year when food is difficult to find. Moreover, the willows created spawning areas and, most importantly, a safe haven from predators. Without these tangles of branches below the water line, the fish become an easy target for populations of cormorants and otters that stalk their prey, then feed remorselessly on their chosen quarry each and every day.

Gary shakes his head, 'They never think of the fish, do they?' he adds, 'Never think of the fish.'

I attempt to lighten his mood with some humour, my usual reaction to stressful situations.

'Remember the old joke about the difference between a good haircut and a bad haircut, Gary?' I ask.

'No, mate.'

'Well, it's two weeks,' I say with a smile. He's not impressed. 'The EA,' I continue, 'tell me that, like a bad haircut, the trees will be back in good order soon. It won't be two weeks though, more like two years.'

'A lot can change in two years,' is his sombre reply, 'there won't be any fish left by then.'

That's true, the fish could have moved to a safer stretch in that time, we just have to hope they don't. Some maintenance is essential if only to remove branches which could detach and then cause blockages at weirs and locks downstream. The amount of pruning the willows have undergone, though, was a great deal more destructive than necessary. A less aggressive approach was required with, perhaps, a selection of trees left untouched until a later date when those which had been pollarded in the initial pruning phase had time to grow. Not only would this have been more aesthetically pleasing, it would also have preserved vital riverside habitat. At least the diesel-powered boats will be able to travel more quickly along this particularly straight stretch of river, more easily overtaking the slower-moving craft and creating a greater volume of wash leading to more erosion and a less habitable waterway for the local fauna. I believe this is classified as an unintended consequence; whether it should have been predicted by the Environment Agency analysts or was completely unexpected, is not something I am qualified to comment on.

The rain continues to pour, it's definitely a double-hat day. (Peaked caps are worn to prevent the hood of a wet weather coat from slipping forward, an issue which seems to apply to all hooded coats designed for fishing.) I squelch over the rain-soaked grass to where Danny is sat under the cover of his boot lid. There's no joking around today, the weather combined with the tree destruction has set a more sober tone.

I have been allotted peg 24, how I wished for this peg back in the warmer days of summer. In a normal winter it can be a productive swim because on the far bank there are two willow trees that form a fish-holding slack. But as I look across the surging river Thames I can no longer see any willow trees, just two bare stumps with no branches and no leaves. There's no slack water, and at present I am struggling to find anywhere that may hold a fish or two. Today will be a tough day, of that I have no doubt. There is a positive though: I am pegged between Leslie and Des, and I could not wish for better company. It also feels like the rain is starting to ease, so while I may not catch today, if the weather improves it'll certainly be an enjoyable morning.

The recent cold snap and heavy rain has changed the appearance of the river. In the summer it looked alive, and it was easy to imagine shoals of fish swimming under the surface searching for food. Now it looks dead and devoid of any life; the river even sounds differently from those warm

July evenings. There's a greater volume of water, of course, but it is the submerged obstructions that cause the rippling sounds as the river, now running much faster, coils itself around the stones, detached tree branches, and other debris that has made its way this far downstream. I have heard these sounds before, during the colder months of seasons past, and they do not prompt memories of nets full of fish. It's time for a coffee while I try to formulate a plan of action.

Three hours into the match and I've not had a bite. The plan, for want of a better description, is not working. Essentially I have adopted an approach that is somewhat less specific than usual: I am simply trying everything I can think of and hoping to get a bite. So far I have experimented with the waggler and stick float at varying distances without as much as a single dip. The feeder rod has been in use: first with a maggot feeder, then a cage feeder, then a range of hook lengths up to four feet long. Still nothing, apart from several willow tree branches. But at least the rain has stopped so it should be dry for the weigh-in, not that I'll be weighing in anything unless my fortunes improve.

Annoyingly, I now have a song stuck in my head. It's going round and round without a break. This means I am not concentrating on fishing, my mind is drifting. It happens often, and it is not just music-related. Suddenly I'll realise that I'm thinking about football, horseracing, data modelling, what I fancy for the evening meal, and why the world is lurching from one disaster to another. There's no surprise that it has happened today, I've not had a single indication of a bite yet, and to be perfectly honest I do not expect to get one. The song that is haunting my thoughts is one I played on the way here in the car: *Tales Of Brave Ulysses* by Cream, and the irony is the lyric that seems to be on a continuous loop is 'Tiny purple fishes, run laughing through your fingers'. I'd certainly settle for a tiny fish at the moment, of any colour come to that from black to bright orange; after all one fish might be enough to win today. Not so many years ago, the Club's Treasurer won the Christmas Match with a single 2oz perch; this stretch of the Thames can be very challenging at times.

Just an hour to go now. The stick float I am using is performing its basic duties admirably: its red tip is perfectly visible against the backdrop and it is keeping the hookbait at any depth I desire. As for the other, more critical, component of its work, so far it has not been called into action in this regard: with no fish in the vicinity of the bait, the float has not registered a single indication of a bite.

In between eating several Bounty bars earlier, Leslie entertained us with the tale of the day he met Her Majesty Queen Elizabeth, and Des recalled the time he was at an auction and bought a racehorse but then realised he had no way of getting it home (fortunately a local racehorse trainer came to his rescue).

My float has just gone under, must be another branch. I can feel movement though, it's not a branch, it's a fish. There are fish out there. The perch is so small it would be better suited to a home aquarium than the mighty river Thames. But I have one in the net and it could be the winner.

Twenty minutes to go and the perch in my net now has a mate, roughly the same size, but Des is connected to something much bigger. His rod is bent to near breaking point as he attempts to lift what appears to be something very heavy up through the watercourse against a current that is doing its best to keep whatever it is safely in the darker depths of the Thames. It's clearly a struggle but through the thin, leafless, branches of the small bush that separates our two pegs I can see him begin to win the battle. The sound of a large splash, and the sight of a landing net being thrust into the river, suggests the fight is drawing to a close.

'Finally!' Des cries.

'Have you got him?' I ask.

'At last, I never thought I'd land that.'

'What is it? A big chub? Or a barbel?'

'No, not quite, it's a TV aerial.'

I decide on a closer inspection. Des is holding the aerial which is not the small loop kind that is attached to a portable television. What Des has in his hands is a full-size television aerial, roughly four feet long, featuring fourteen pairs of elements, a driver, and over six feet of cable. It should be attached to the roof or chimney stack of a house somewhere.

'I know the floods were deep last winter, but this is a bit much,' Des remarks with a smile.

By the final whistle I had added nothing more to my collection of fish, and both Leslie and Des were drying their nets on the bank ready for the journey home. My earlier optimism, based on the premise that no one had caught, has been somewhat tempered. Apparently plenty of fish have been banked downstream. It looks like Danny has decided not to stop and is walking straight past with the scales.

'Aren't you going to weigh me in?' I ask.

'You haven't caught anything,' he replies and keeps walking.

'That's where you're wrong,' I add.

'If you've caught then you're the only one along this bit who has,' he says clearly doubting my claim.

'Set the scales up and give me a hand with the net, it could be heavy.'

'If you're winding me up I won't be happy.'

I begin to lift the net, ring by ring, 'Get the weigh sling ready, Danny,' I call out. It's surprising how long a keepnet measuring over fourteen feet in length takes to get in when you're taking your time just for effect.

'Get a move on, Pete.'

'Here we go,' I lift the net clear of the bank and carry it over. I know the fish are small, but surrounded by so much netting they look even tinier. Danny laughs, 'Was it worth it?'

'Just get them on the scales, Daniel,' I reply, adopting a most imperious tone.

Danny carefully examines the dial. 'Two ounces, that do you?'

It's more than I expected, but not a great return for so much effort. The six of us drawn in the section facing the tree stumps had a tough day, in fact my two little fish were the only ones to make it into a net. Those fishing downstream where the trees remain undisturbed, for now, did much better, with chub to over 4lbs and some nice roach landed. As I make my way back to the car I cannot help but wonder whether our failure is a portent of what we might have to endure in the next couple of seasons before the trees finally return to their former glory. I certainly hope not, otherwise the PAC could lose a significant proportion of its members and may no longer be financially viable – another unintended consequence. On the plus side, at least Des now has a spare TV aerial.

When fishing the upper reaches of the Thames it is easy to forget that, just a short distance downstream, this narrow, rather unimposing channel becomes the vast open stretch of water that was arguably the most important waterway in the formation of the nation. The history of the Thames, in all of its reaches, is intertwined with the history of England: Britons, Romans, Saxons, the Nordic Peoples and the Normans all made it their 'seat of war' and during times of peace made its banks the heart of countless settlements.

It is astounding to think that as humans took their first tentative steps northwards across the vast landmass of Europe, before the British Isles broke away, they would eventually arrive at the banks of the river Thames. Their natural instincts would have told them that they had found the ideal place to settle. Not only was the river a defensive barrier against possible invaders, human or animal, it also provided drinking water and a means to cleanse bodies and to wash wounds. Most importantly, however, the river became an invaluable source of food.

Although it is doubtful that any of the ancient people, when contemplating an over-hanging willow tree or reed bed, thought 'If I trotted a piece of bread flake along that glide I'd have a good chance of catching a chub.' Yet, it is perfectly conceivable that by strategically organising many of their community, and possibly using some kind of rudimentary net, they would have been able to corral fish for easier capture in what was a much shallower, wider, river. A ready-made food source was critical to the creation of any settlement, large or small. So too was safety during this period in history when death came all too easily. With the river on one side, a human lookout and an arrangement of fires to ward off the unwanted attentions of wild animals on another, a dwelling near to the river would be well protected from the dangers that lurked in the dense forests that covered southern England at the time.

Of course in those Neolithic times the Thames would not have had a name, or if it did it was not recorded. While there is still a certain amount of disagreement about the origins of its name, the word *Thames* was most likely derived from the Brittonic word *Tamesas,* a term in use during the Iron Age. In fact, the root of this word appears in many other British rivers including the Tame, Tamar, and Tavy. This alone seems a justification for *Tamesas* to be the source. Much later, the Victorians gave the river a second name: *Isis.* This was used for the upper reaches, with the name changing to Thames after its confluence with the river Thame near Dorchester.

Julius Caesar certainly referred to the river as the Thames, although he used the Latin equivalent, during his second visit in 54BC. He also noted with dismay that the watercourse caused a major obstacle to his progress. According to his own observations at the time, the river could only be forded at one place, and even then it was with great difficulty. This gave the tribes that inhabited its banks, such as the Cassivellanus, a great advantage in combat situations. Ultimately, though, the overwhelming power and military expertise of the Roman invading forces enabled them to colonise England for over 400 years.

Though more advanced than the Britons in many ways, the Romans did learn a valuable lesson from both the indigenous population and the difficulties they encountered during their invasion. As a result, Roman settlements and fortifications were sited along the river, the biggest of which was Londinium. While undoubtedly useful in battle situations, rivers do cause issues in everyday life. For a population to function at maximum efficiency, a basic principle of the Roman way of life, easy access from one bank to the other was essential. Bridges needed to be built and fortunately the Romans had the skills to do it. Archaeological evidence suggests that the first permanent crossing of the Thames was built in Londinium around 50AD in the region now known as Southwark. It remained in use for many decades and part of its structure is still visible today.

In the centuries that followed, the Thames gained importance in every facet of life. Even *Magna Carta* was signed on the banks of (or possibly on an island in) the river Thames. Although no longer quite such a crucial component for defence purposes, the river became essential to trade. SC Hall wrote in the *Book of the Thames* (1877):

'[from] the meadow by Trewsbury Mead – its lonely birthplace – through its whole course, gathering tributaries, and passing with them through tranquil villages, populous towns, and crowded cities; ever fertilizing, ever beautifying, ever enriching, until it reaches the most populous city of the modern or ancient world, forming thence the GREAT HIGHWAY by which a hundred nations traverse the globe.'

Naturally the growing importance of the river attracted more and more people to the Thames Valley and London in particular. Rapid population increase is never good for natural resources both at a local and global level. Infrastructure is always one or two steps behind, and this was the case with England's greatest river. As early as the fourteenth century this vital body of water that stretched from the Cotswolds to the Essex coast was suffering from the impact of an ever-growing population. Essentially the Thames was viewed as a natural sewer. By the mid 1800s, it had turned toxic with the most polluted area found within the capital itself. Four cholera outbreaks, resulting from the build up of bacteria in the watercourse that provided an essential source of drinking water, caused the death of many thousands of residents who lived and worked along the banks of the Thames. Immediate action was required.

It was Joseph Bazalgette who saved the city from drowning in its own sewage. Under his guidance an extensive sewer network was constructed. Over eight miles of underground sewers were built, along with more than a thousand miles of street sewers. No longer would the streets and thoroughfares of London be filled with the stench of rotting offal and untreated sewage. His wondrous construction was officially opened in 1865 although it was a decade later before the project was finally completed.

While this solved the problems encountered in the capital, the worst affected area, it did nothing for the less urbanised regions. The next step in the attempt to clean Britain's rivers was the *River Pollution Prevention Act* (1876), which remained the basis of the legislation for protecting the waterways until a new act was introduced in 1951. George Sclater-Booth MP, as President of the Local Government Board in Disraeli's administration, was ultimately responsible for the 1876 Act's implementation. When challenged about its effectiveness he replied rather obliquely that the most important outcome of the Act had been the 'prevention of *fresh* pollution of rivers' adding 'no loan for sewerage works is now sanctioned unless provision is made for the purification of the sewage.' Unfortunately, this bold declaration, outlining the good intentions of this Act, no longer seems to be applicable. Almost 150 years after the Act was first introduced, Water Companies are now permitted by law to discharge raw sewage into the waterways of the nation providing they alert the relevant authorities of their intentions. It seems that little progress has been made in this area in which significant change is required.

Historically the Thames had been seen as an important defensive barrier whether protecting one ancient tribe from another or the entire country from invaders from overseas such as the Romans and the Vikings. This fact would not have been on many people's minds during the first half of the twentieth century, but in the early days of the Second World War it was at the forefront of discussions between the military commanders and the politicians in Whitehall. The Allied offensive effort in France was failing, with British troops pushed back to the beaches of Dunkirk. In the scramble to evacuate as many men as possible, huge amounts of equipment had to be sacrificed. As a result an exhausted, under-equipped British Army faced the prospect of an imminent German invasion. In these dark days, the senior military officials decided to construct a system of defences across southern England. It was hoped that these would halt, or at least slow, the German advance. The Thames was to be an integral part of the defensive structure. Along its length, pillboxes were built in rapid time such was the fear. These complimented the strategically placed tank traps, high ground lookout posts, road blocks, fortified houses, and companies of soldiers, including the Royal Marines, who were stationed at what were considered to be the more critical sites along the line.

Fortunately, due to the efforts of the Royal Air Force, the invasion was averted and these defensive mechanisms were not called into action. Over seventy years later, many of the concrete structures remain. Anyone who has fished the Thames at Sutton Courtenay (the site of a former Roman settlement) will be well aware of the pillbox that continues to keep a watchful eye on the river not far from the bridge.

As well as providing the inhabitants of southern England with a plentiful supply of food and water, alongside being a natural defensive barrier, this slender ribbon of water has, not surprisingly, inspired countless artists, poets, and writers.

Artists from around the globe have been fascinated by the Thames ever since a method of making a permanent record of a visual image was discovered. After the Thirty Years War forced Wenceslaus Hollar out of Prague, he made many European countries his home before moving to England in 1637. In the midst of the English Civil War he created the now famous *Long View of London*, a panoramic depiction of the city with the Thames running snake-like through the centre of the etching. Hollar was among many artists enchanted by the river.

James Whistler did not only paint portraits of his family. The American artist clearly had affection for London, the city he adopted as his home, and he painted several views of the Thames during his years in England including a haunting lithograph of the river at Battersea.

Other artists who committed the Thames to canvas included Canaletto, Edward Dayes, JMW Turner, Claude Monet, Samuel Scott, and William Marlow. Although most of these concentrated on the capital, a few, including Turner, ventured upstream with the smaller towns and cities, locks, weirs and bridges being the main focal points of their work.

A great many yards of poetry have been written about the Thames over the centuries and a range of descriptive terms used in an attempt to bring the river to life on the printed page. Colours are critical in such descriptions and have often been incorporated into verse. The Thames, though, presents a difficult problem in this regard with even the shortest glide featuring a range of colours and hews that varies almost hour to hour and certainly will appear very different from one day to the next. Thacker (1920) opted for 'grey' when describing the river in flood. Others chose brighter tones for their work, including such descriptive terms as 'silver', 'glittering', 'sparkling', and 'silver-streaming'. With respect to character, in the poet's eye the Thames can be 'sleepy', 'winding', 'shy', 'stripling', or, according to Michael Drayton's topographical poem *Poly-Olbion* dating from 1622, 'fair and goodly'. In *The Burden Of Itys*, Oscar Wilde chose to describe the movement of the river. His phrase 'The Thames creeps on in sluggish leadenness' is quite apt for the lower reaches of the river.

From an angler's perspective, especially one who adopts a more relaxed approach to fishing, one of the most memorable verses was penned by the Poet Laureate Robert Seymour Bridges in 1890 in his poem *There is a Hill*. He describes how an angler casts out his line into the 'silver Thames' then, leaning against a tree, starts to read his book and falls asleep while *'curious fishes peel About his nibbled bait, or scornfully Dart off and rise and leap'*.

Many anglers like to meet the challenge which the great rivers of Britain pose, whether or not they have been rendered on canvas or portrayed in eloquent poetic verse. The Ouse, Trent and Wye easily make this classification along with several others. I would suggest the upper and lower reaches of the Thames would not be out of place on such a list, and not just for the quality of fishing. After all, to cast a line on to the river Thames is, to borrow a phrase from the eminent politician John Burns, to cast a line into 'liquid history'.

CHAPTER 7

SHOULD HAVE BEEN A PHOTO FINISH

*Fishing with a new club; other anglers' unusual bait
preferences; fishing photography; perch.*

This morning I am travelling northwards to a match at a venue
not controlled by the PAC. Fishing against a different group
of anglers is not only challenging but is also very informative.
I'm hoping to pick up some tips that will come in handy when
I am back on home territory. The lake on which the match
will be fished is packed with carp up to about 20lbs, a few
bream, hundreds of roach and some nice perch. Although I
have caught many carp from this venue in the past, I won't be
targeting them this morning. Today's contest is divided into
two parts: silver fish and carp, with a payout for the highest

and second highest weights in each division. It is sure to attract some top class carp matchmen against whom I would stand little chance of success, so my focus will be the silvers. Hopefully the carp will not be as troublesome as the bleak can be on the river.

Whilst the lake is stocked along the lines of a commercial, it is very different in other ways. Originally it was a gravel pit. Oxfordshire is well known for gravel extraction, with records showing that gravel from the Thames flood plain has been utilised for building projects in many locations across southern England since the late Middle Ages. Gravel is the accumulation of river beds over thousands of years – the changing course of the Thames, as well as its tributaries, is the main reason so much of the aggregate can be found in the county. The pit we are fishing today is not quite as ancient as many of the other gravel workings in the region, with excavation not undertaken until the late twentieth century.

When excavating neighbouring pits several surprising finds were made. At one location, just a few hundred yards from where today's match will take place, the extraction process had to be halted when a large bone-like object was unearthed. The find created a great deal of excitement in academic circles with archaeologists confirming it to be the tusk from a mammoth dating from around 200,000 years BC. Further investigations uncovered a range of bones from a selection of other animals including wolves, bears, lions, elephants and bison.

Clearly, given the presence of animals usually found in more temperate climes, the climate in the county would have been vastly different at that time. More strangely, though, amongst these skeletal remains, other artefacts were found that proved that an animal of a greater intelligence co-existed with these wild beasts, specifically Neanderthals. A little shorter, but thicker-set and more muscular than early modern humans, Neanderthals are known to have lived in Europe from around 400,000 years to about 40,000 BC. Given the constant threat they faced from these wild animals it is surprising they survived for so long. At least they had plenty of food: their diet of 80% meat would easily have been satisfied with the capture of one or two mammoths which stood up to 13 feet tall at the shoulder.

Whenever I get snagged up while fishing one of the lakes on this particular complex, I assume that it's weed, or more likely a tree branch. There is the possibility, though, that I am connected to something much older and much more intriguing. To date, I have yet to land anything resembling a lion's tooth or mammoth's tusk, but there's always the chance of catching something exotic when fishing a venue that was once an archaeological hot spot, even when the fish are not feeding.

Disappointingly, in recent years many of Oxfordshire's gravel pits have been used for landfill. Some had been stocked with fish and were a valuable resource to the local community. Even so, several of these were later reclaimed by their owners and filled with discarded waste such as ash from a local power station. Fortunately, in the 1980s a group of forward-thinking anglers from Witney purchased a small number of these lakes which have been preserved for future generations of anglers to enjoy.

Today the weather is mild, at least it is for the time of year. The sun is holding the upper-hand and will maintain the temperature at a pleasant level until obscured by the woolpack clouds that are gathering on the horizon. There have been a few frosts recently that chilled the air a little too much for most pleasure anglers, so the lake has not seen a great deal of angling pressure during the past week which is an added bonus. With the car unloaded and my pools money paid, I make my way to the group of anglers who are waiting for the draw to commence. I recognise a few faces, but do not know anyone by name. Two anglers towards the outside of the main cluster seem quite sociable, so I stroll in their direction. The one doing most of the talking is fairly rotund, with a round face, and is much younger than the average age of the other match anglers. His companion is older, greyer, and apparently missing most of his teeth. I nod and smile when they make eye contact, 'Nice day for it,' I say in my cheeriest tone.

'It'll be a hard day,' the older one replies, 'but that's okay, better than sitting at home.' The younger angler is leaning on his barrow. Hanging off the handle is a bucket full of boilies, more than I'd use in a whole season.

'Wow, that's a lot of boilies,' I say pointing to the bucket.

'Honeycomb flavour.' He puts his hand into the bucket and gets a handful out. 'Try one.'

'You're ok, I'll stick to my sandwiches.'

'No, honestly, they're lovely,' and with that he throws one in my direction, and pops another into his mouth.

As I smell the spherical bait I'm surprised by how pungent it is, unmistakably honey-based. In fact it is quite a pleasant smell, very sweet, and somewhat appealing. Sweetened baits have been used in carp fishing for many hundreds of years. In the 17th century, Izaak Walton recommended using 'the crumbs of bread and honey, made into a paste'. The base mix of modern boilies tends to produce a firmer more resilient foundation for the flavouring than bread crumbs, otherwise there is little to separate the two approaches.

I throw the boilie back into the bucket, 'We don't want you running out,' I say laughing but essentially just wanting to put some distance between me and the item I was clearly expected to eat and enjoy.

He grins at me, 'I think I have enough for today.'

'It's cat meat for me,' says the older of the two, his lack of teeth even more apparent as his face became animated. Using cat meat for bait was popular a few years ago, especially the soft chunky varieties. It is far less common to see it used on the bank nowadays mainly due to the awful smell that is seemingly immovable from any surface this most appalling foodstuff touches.

'Oh, right,' I reply, 'so cat meat down the edge for carp I suppose. On the pole, or rod?' It's one of my many habits to end a comment with a question since it almost guarantees a continuation of the conversation. I never feel comfortable standing around in silence.

'No,' he replies, 'I mean to eat. I just can't resist it; once I start I can't stop.'

Now there's silence and it is uncomfortable for so many reasons. He looks sincere, but surely he isn't. He's not smiling and I can feel my lower jaw beginning to drop, which is not something that happens often. I'm staring at his face, searching for a hint that he is winding me up. Nothing, not even the slightest intimation that he is joking. The air remains heavy with silence and I switch my gaze to the younger angler. He looks unperturbed by the comment, nonchalant even. A few more seconds pass, neither dissolve into laughter, there has been no 'gotcha' moment. Maybe he's serious; maybe he actually eats cat meat. I know anglers who eat their cheese, luncheon meat, or even their sweetcorn straight from the tin, but not cat meat. Surely not cat meat.

'Oh, er, okay, I see, right.' No matter how hard I try, I cannot find the correct words to respond coherently. Are there any correct words for this situation? 'That conjures up an image guaranteed to leave no stomach unchurned' would possibly fit the bill, but instead I remain silent. He turns to the younger member of our group, finally there would be an admission that it was all just a joke. But no, instead he asks him which side of the lake he'd prefer to draw as if we were in the middle of a 'normal' conversation and there wasn't an unresolved issue hanging in the air.

'Far side, definitely, or peg 1.' They both look my way inviting a response. Clearly the conversation has moved on, which leaves me a little dumbfounded.

'Oh, I don't mind, I'm after the silvers,' I stutter still trying to process what I've just heard and still not entirely sure they are not just having me on.

'Come on, draw,' a voice from behind me finally breaks the awkwardness, at least it was awkward for me, the others seem to be quite comfortable about the prospect of eating cat meat.

I have been allotted peg 8; it's on the nearside bank and I am more than happy with it. The only downside is that I am the only angler in the match with competitors on both adjacent pegs, and both of them happen to be good silver fish anglers. Of course, a better draw would have been next to my new toothless acquaintance. That would have resolved so many issues as well as satisfying my curiosity as to what he'll have for his lunch: a tin of chicken and duck with added gravy possibly, or maybe something from the gourmet range featuring tuna and lamb. More likely it would be cheese sandwiches then I'd at least know for certain I had been the victim of a wind-up.

One way this lake differs from conventional commercial fisheries is the depth. A couple of metres from the bank it is already at four feet deep, at thirteen metres on some pegs, including this one, it is over twelve feet deep. Despite that, many standard commercial fishery approaches work for the carp anglers, including the method feeder and pellet waggler close to the island which runs through the centre of the venue. My plan is to fish a feeder, a long pole line, a short pole line and a margin line for the perch. Where I normally put the perch line, the water is very clear; in fact I can see every stone, leaf, and twig on the lake bed. So I think I'll put that one out a little further into the lake, at least then I won't be able to see that I'm fishing in an area devoid of fish.

Three hours into the match now. The anglers either side of me have yet to get an indication and I have had only one bite: a carp took a fancy to my double pinkie hookbait on the long pole line. Despite using only a 2lbs hook length it was the pole elastic that gave way, much to my surprise. The dacron connector seemingly cut through the Middy Shockcore 6-10 elastic like a cheese wire through a mature cheddar. It's fair to say that the match is not going well. A robin that continually flits from tree to pole to bait box is enjoying a good feast of maggots though.

My peg protrudes into the lake by about four feet. To my left a jack pike of about 7lbs lies motionless in the clear marginal water. He's completely unperturbed by my presence, but nonetheless decides to try a more productive area of the lake. Clearly, he does not feel I will be catching any silver fish that he can steal. So with a gentle flick of his tail, he swims away in a stately fashion displaying an air of utter supremacy and seemingly total disgust at my failure to provide him with brunch.

To my right lies a decaying bed of reeds that would have looked a great deal more attractive as a fish-holding area in the summer. Now they are pale in colour, less dense, and collapsing forward into the water. Just beyond the reeds a willow tree extends a few, spindly, leafless branches across the surface, admittedly offering some cover, but hardly enough to shelter a shoal of fish. Something in the back of my mind is telling me to consider the dying reeds more closely.

Where I have set the perch line is rather in 'no man's land' in that it isn't at the bottom of the shelf where food may collect, nor close to any form of cover that would act as a good ambush point for a perch. I seem to remember, many years ago, someone explaining how the banks of this lake are undercut. If they are, then maybe there's a predator, in the shape of a big perch lying in the shelter the bank provides, waiting for unsuspecting fry to swim past. I'll drop some worms tight to the reeds, under that branch and give it a go.

I've just shortened my perch rig so that the float is less than six inches from the pole tip; any longer and I risk the possibility of it tangling with the willow tree branches when fishing my new spot which is, essentially, my last hope. Even so, getting the bait sufficiently close to the bank will not be easy, and getting it back will be just as difficult because I'm sure there's a snag or two where I hope the fish will be, possibly even a mammoth's tusk.

The rig is now in place. If it fails to produce then I may be on my way home early, but if there is a fish hiding under the reeds then I'll know pretty soon. In fact I know already, the float is slowly sliding under the lake surface – the most enjoyable and exciting sight in fishing. Count to three, strike, and hope for some decent resistance.

'One...two...three...' here we go. It feels solid, but not a snag, finally I'm into a good fish, I just have to extricate him from his lair without coiling the rig around the willow branches, or allowing him to dive further into the cover that will surely end the fight prematurely. I'm making progress, the fish is away from the danger area, but I wish I had used a solid elastic with less stretch because he's now making his way back to the willow. A puller kit would help by allowing me to shorten the elastic and gain greater control, but I don't have one on this top-two. Keep the pressure on. He's in open water now. Finally I have control. At first sight he looks like a very big perch; big for me anyway. As I slide the net under him I breathe a sigh of relief, at least I am weighing-in today.

Just thirty minutes to go now. The angler to my right has had one fish, around two ounces, the one to my left has had two decent perch, and I've added about six ounces of fish to the net, all from the long pole line. Disappointingly, my newly designated perch line has not produced any more bites.

With the match over, I can see the Match Secretary approaching with the scales. Apparently the silvers have not shown in any great numbers today; one angler has found some bream, but the others have struggled.

I have just been told that my perch is a shade under 3lbs, which is a shame because I was convinced it was a three-pounder. My total weight is not quite enough to get a payout, but that one big fish is enough to make the day a success.

Perch really are stunning fish and I'm going to have one last look before returning him to the lake.

'Want a photo, mate?' I briefly consider the offer, then decline. Over the years I have accumulated very few fishing photos for three main reasons.

First, I am not particularly photogenic. Photographs of many PAC members such as Leslie, Danny, and Phil, a good friend who no longer fishes matches, always come out flawlessly. I suspect they must possess some indeterminate facial attribute that makes a crucial difference. An increased degree of symmetry maybe, or a head shape that is more favourable when it comes to photographic replication. Whatever it is, their images are without exception perfectly mirrored by the camera's lens. For me, it is very different. Invariably, as I look towards the photographer, my face takes on a weirdly contorted expression, about which I am totally unaware. When I get to see the photos I always wonder quite how I was able to twist my features into such an unappealing form. To make matters worse, my often bizarre appearance completely distracts from the focal point of the image: the fish. As a result, most photographs of my catches tend to be accompanied by a headless angler as I attempt to improve them with a little photo-editing.

Second, my style of fishing is more geared to volume than one or two top quality specimens, so I tend not to catch that many fish worthy of a photograph. Even when I do get a decent roach of a couple of pounds, or perch nearing three as in the match, a tench over seven pounds, or bleak pushing three ounces, and agree to a photograph, the fish always look so much smaller on film than they do on the bank. This somewhat mystical distortion in the fabric of time and space that affects cameras also applies to a keepnet. During a match

I can regularly fill my net with good-sized roach, only to find that they have magically shrunk to just average size at the weigh-in. It's a phenomenon that not even the combined intelligence of Albert Einstein and Stephen Hawking would have been able to explain.

Finally, I do not possess a mobile phone with a built-in camera. Many years ago I was the proud owner of an Olympus Trip (for younger readers an Olympus Trip was a camera that the photographer filled with film, took photographs, and when the film was used removed the roll from the camera, sent it away, then waited for a fortnight to get the exposed images back). It must have been a good camera because it was advertised by David Bailey (for younger readers David Bailey was the most well-know fashion photographer of the era and was responsible for many iconic photographs of The Beatles, England footballers, and various fashion models). The camera was safely stored in my fishing bag, and hardly ever saw the light of day. It suffered from the extreme heat of the summer, to the cold of winter, but when called into action, it still produced excellent photographs, unless I was in them. Unfortunately I did not use it that often and film rolls normally consisted of 24 frames, so it would take me, literally, years to use them all. By the time the negatives had been developed and returned to me, I had forgotten about most of the fish that appeared on them.

As I watch the perch swim happily away I'm already regretting not taking up the offer of a photograph. Why does that happen immediately after the point at which the decision cannot be reversed? The perch was a spectacular fish, my biggest for many years. It deserved a photo which would have been a nice reminder in the future, even if it was in the hands of a headless angler.

The cat meat enthusiast had a poorer day than most. Apparently he had forgotten to take a tin opener, so not only did he have to fish with alternative bait, he had nothing for lunch – well that's what I was told!

According to many anglers, the gravel pit where the match was held is home to some very big perch. On many occasions I have had conversations with anglers returning to their cars after a day's fishing and they have told me, in matter of fact fashion, about the giants they landed earlier in the day, mostly over 3lbs. I have yet to see one on the bank that can match these claims though. The one I caught in the match, at a little under 3lbs, is the largest perch I have seen. That is not to say there aren't bigger specimens in the lake. One angler who I know weighs his fish very diligently did tell me about a 3-pounder he caught, which is all the evidence I need to be confident they do exist. However, I am not so sure about the accuracy of the weight of the fish for which 'estimates' are used. Perch seem to be a species of fish which appear to be heavier than they actually weigh. This is possibly connected to the shape of the fish. Their colouration, big eyes, deep bodies, and large spiny dorsal fin make them look much bigger than they are and can easily lead to overestimation. This in not a new phenomenon, even the earliest angling writers were fooled by this most impressive of fish.

Writing in 1893, H Cholmondeley-Pennel recalls the largest specimen he witnessed: a preserved fish in a case on the wall of a small Perthshire inn. The accompanying information suggested that the fish weighed 7lbs, and the writer concluded that 'it certainly could not have weighed less than five or six.' He then lists a selection of specimen perch with three assessed at 8lbs; these were apparently taken from the Serpentine, Wiltshire Avon, and Dagenham Reach in Essex. A perch weighing 8lbs caught in an English river would most definitely be a fish of a lifetime.

SC and AM Hall mention in their book of 1877 that fish of 5lbs are frequently caught in the Thames, with specimens of 'eight or nine pounds' banked on occasion. These rather fanciful weights would make the largest fish around 50% heavier than the current UK perch record and more likely a product of either very inaccurate scales or an over active imagination.

Not to be out done, Izaak Walton also writes about a huge perch caught by Sir Abraham Williams. An 'honest informer' told Walton that the fish in question was 'almost two feet long'. This led Walton to speculate further about what this enormous perch may have preyed upon. His conclusion was that this leviathan would 'have devoured a pike of half his own length.'

Maybe it is for these reasons that Richard Walker referred to the perch as 'the biggest of all fish'.

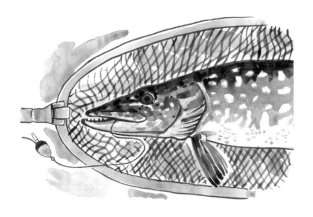

CHAPTER 8

BEGINNER'S LUCK OR RAW TALENT?

Predators; issues with clothing;
mythical fish; predation.

The river is just coming into sight. It's a frosty, bright morning and for once the car is not full with fishing tackle: there's no pole or whip, no pole rollers, no keepnet, no bait bag. Today I have two rods, a tackle bag, unhooking mat, comfortable chair, landing net and a small pouch of bait. The reason for this reduction in kit is a simple one: today's contest is a pike match. I have never fished one of these before, and I am pretty sure that today's contest is the first of its kind held by the PAC.

It's a few years since I fished for the most eminent of toothy predators, which has presented its own problems. Normally I just load my gear into the back of the car and I'm away; for this event I had to climb into the loft and dust off some rods and reels I had not used for some considerable time. Also, I had to construct a new set of wire traces just in case a pike grabs my bait; find some suitable floats; and buy a pack of sardines. Despite this sizeable additional workload about which I complained most vehemently to the Match Secretary in mock frustration, I am very much looking forward to the challenge this unique match poses. Danny's considered response to my moaning was as cutting as ever: 'You don't know what real work is, all you do is press a few keys and scratch a pen across paper.' Actually, he's not far wrong there.

The match format is quite different to our usual competitions. There is a draw but that is restricted to pegs 15 to 26. After two hours of fishing, the match will be suspended and each angler asked, in turn starting with the person on the highest draw, whether or not he/she would like to move pegs. If a move is requested then the angler has the choice to fish any unused peg from 2 to 14 for the remaining two hours of the match. If I get the opportunity, I'll move to peg 8. A large reed bed grows a little downstream from that peg and it is sure to have a predator somewhere nearby.

According to Izaak Walton, the pike, or 'fresh-water wolf', possesses a 'bold, greedy, devouring disposition'. This is true to a certain extent: they are definitely bold. In a nearby lake the pike lie unseen under the fishing platforms. They expend little energy in their hideaway and wait patiently, not for an assuming prey fish to swim by, but for the angler above them to provide their meal. After a while, the angler may start to catch silver fish, but again the pike just wait; they don't rush to grab the first one they see because that would mean a battle they want to avoid. Instead they sit motionless under the cover of the platform until the angler releases the fish back into the lake. Then, with the speed of an express train, they dart from their ambush point and grab the unsuspecting fish. Maximum return for minimum effort – and no chance of being caught. The ferocity with which they take the fish, invariably on the lake's surface, and the closeness this strike can be to vulnerable finger tips, often causes the angler's heart rate to momentarily jump – it certainly does mine. On this evidence alone the pike is clearly an exceptionally intelligent fish. I just hope the river fish are not quite so on the ball as their stillwater relatives. If they are they may wonder what a headless saltwater sardine is doing in the Upper Thames.

With the match just underway I have started to put my well-founded plan into action. I intend to wobble a deadbait (cast out and slowly retrieve the sardine) for a while, to search as much of the peg as possible, then put the static bait into what I feel would be a good ambush point for a pike. Surely it's a plan that can only succeed?

The combination of their considerable size and jaws lined with needle sharp teeth, has earned the pike a reputation of almost mythical proportions. Often, when newcomers to a venue meet anglers who have been fishing the water for more years than they care to remember, they will be told, in hushed tones, of a particular pike that lurks under the surface. Invariably these fish are of enormous dimensions, capable of swallowing a mallard in a single gulp, and possess the meanest of demeanours with the darkest of eyes that give them the most menacing of appearances. While these beasts are seen, they are never caught. As a teenager I fished a small

Thames tributary, mostly for chub and roach, and it was not long before I became acquainted with the legend of the monster pike. On a cold winter's day back in the early 1980s, after a brief chat with the Bailiff, he paused and started to stroke his greying beard thoughtfully as if he was deciding whether or not to let me in on a secret. I waited patiently as there was clearly a significant pronouncement coming. Finally he looked me straight in the eye, and in the gravest of tones said 'Do you know about the big pike?' Much to his delight, I shook my head by way of a response, inviting him to tell his tale. Apparently, this monster that patrolled the river 'just below the ford so don't slip when you are crossing to the other bank' was so big that it was able to break the strongest line as easily as it would lightweight cotton, and on some occasions evaded capture by smashing landing nets. So revered was the pike that it was given a name. Oddly the fish, that would no doubt have been female (if it existed), was referred to as 'Big Bert'. I cannot attest to the accuracy of this particular tale, but it did inspire me to buy some piking gear.

Despite my best efforts I never connected with 'Big Bert', although whenever I fished that stretch of the river, especially when the daylight was fading, each time my pike float bobbed it did cross my mind that I may soon be connected, and might become the first to land, the duck-eating, net-breaking leviathan that ruled the watery domain just below the ford.

My efforts today have been just as futile: wobbling did not produce a single take, so just now I switched to deadbaiting, and a short while ago the float did indeed bob a little. It wasn't 'Big Bert' – not even mythical pike can live that long. More likely it was a crayfish, not what I am after today.

Pike mythology is not restricted to Great Britain. Like the fish itself, tales of monster pike can be found in all corners of the northern hemisphere. One of the most unusual originated in Scandinavia. Writing in *Scandinavian Adventures* (Volume 1), Llewelyn Lloyd recounts a tale told to him by an acquaintance 'in whose word I [Lloyd] place every reliance'. Apparently three companions were accompanied on a fishing trip to a large lake in Fryksdal by an experienced local fisherman referred to only as Modin. While long-lining on the lake, Modin suddenly redirected the craft off their intended route so violently as to cause concern. He then began to row 'with all his might to shore'. When questioned about this abrupt and unexpected change of plan, he merely pointed out into the lake and with some alarm in his voice muttered 'Sjö Troll'. Stories of the Sjö Troll, an evil water sprite, were well known to the others who quickly turned their attention to the area of the lake Modin had claimed he had seen the beast. From out of the mist which seemed to float over the placid water like a spectral cloud, there came into view an apparition that none would have expected: a quite hideous form, more suited to land than water. The three companions were staring in disbelief as 'something greatly resembling the horns of an elk, or reindeer' was cutting through the surface at speed. In one terrifying instant it became clear that the Sjö Troll was not just another tale from Scandinavian folklore, but a living, breathing creature.

Convinced what they were witnessing had earthly origins, and was not from the realm of pixies and goblins, all except Modin were determined to get a closer look. After no little cajoling from his passengers, the oarsman reluctantly changed course again, this time, against his better judgement, rowing towards the demon. Once within range, a member of the party drew his pistol and fired a shot in the direction of the Sjö Troll; his aim was true and the four men, with trembling hands and more than just a degree of trepidation, were able to wrestle the beast into the boat. To their great relief their prize was not some previously unidentified monster capable of sinking the small craft, instead it was a huge pike. As for the horns they witnessed raking through the surface of the lake, these were the skeletal remains of an eagle. The pike was so powerful that when attacked by the bird she was able to dive and stay submerged long enough to ensure the eagle was drowned. Over time the carcass of the bird began to rot, the flesh and feathers fell away, and all that remained was the bones protruding from the pike's back. It was sightings of this curious shape that gave rise to the local tale of the lake being haunted by a Sjö Troll.

While watching a leafless branch of a willow tree sail along the Thames, at least I think it is a branch, I notice Danny making his way to the hedgerow; obviously he needs to answer a call of nature. I suppose I could quickly hide his sardines and leave a note saying 'Thanks for the fish, we'll have them on toast tonight', but that would be a little unfair.

With no indications that a pike is anywhere near my deadbait, I have decided to move it. As I swing the sardine to hand, a young child's voice makes me turn.

'Look, Dad, he's caught one.'

'Well done!' his father adds, 'that's the first fish we have seen caught today.'

'Um, well, it's actually my bait, not a fish capture.'

'Oh, sorry.'

As the pair continue their Sunday morning walk, I hear a muffled cry of anguish and frustration from the direction of the hedgerow. Anticipating the Match Secretary's actions is often far from easy, but even with a hundred guesses at my disposal I would not have predicted the scene I am now witnessing. Danny, for some inexplicable reason, is lying on the ground pulling violently at one of his boots. It doesn't look like he's taken a tumble; his actions are far too animated for someone recovering from a fall. So, what is he trying to achieve? Now he's attacking the other boot with the same degree of ferocity. Why though? Both boots are now off and he appears to be trying to remove his trousers. This is becoming a little worrying. Maybe there's a simple reason such as an errant wasp infiltrating his clothing. Maybe it's more complex: perhaps Danny's actions are the physical manifestation of some emotional crisis and soon he'll be running up and down the bank fully naked. If it's the latter, I'll just look the other way and if anyone asks I'll pretend not to know him. For now I'll focus on fishing and await the consequences.

Several minutes have now passed, and Danny has still not returned to his peg. Thankfully I can rule out the more concerning of the two explanations I formulated earlier. But I cannot ignore the situation any longer, I'll have to check on him. Shifting my gaze from float to hedgerow I can, with no small amount of relief, see Danny walking back across the field to the river. Better still, he is fully clothed.

'What was all that about, Danny?'

'Boots wouldn't come off,' he replies matter-of-factly as if that's sufficient explanation.

'I could see that, but why were you taking your boots off?'

'I can't get my trousers off over my boots can I?' his frustration is clear at what, to him at least, seems like a facetious question. Although the conversation is taking a rather tortuous route, I'll have to persevere just to satisfy my own curiosity. So I'll try again: 'Why were you taking your trousers off, Danny?' If he says he cannot get his underpants off without removing his trousers I'll bring the interrogation to an immediate halt.

'Well, I put my waterproof trousers on back to front, didn't I, the zip was at the back.'

'Oh, I see,' I reply failing to suppress a smile.

'I thought something's been sticking into me all morning. It was the zip,' he adds disgruntledly, then cracks a smile himself. I've made a mental note that in future, under similar circumstances, I simply won't ask.

The whistle has just sounded for the end of the match, and all I have caught is a crayfish. Even the move to peg 8, the spot I thought was bound to produce a pike, was entirely fruitless. A pike has been banked, though. A short while ago Gary landed a 7lbs specimen. Not the biggest pike in the Thames, but a significant achievement for Gary who has never fished for pike before. The rest of the match anglers called it 'beginner's luck', Gary preferred 'raw talent'. Whatever it was, Gary is now well and truly hooked on pike fishing and there's little doubt that the tackle he purchased especially for the Pike Match will see plenty of use over the coming months. This alone has made the day a success.

Pike may be the supreme ambush predators, but they are far from alone when it comes to the predation of fish in the rivers, lakes and canals of Britain. And, unfortunately, not all predators are good for the ecosystem they inhabit.

The signal crayfish was introduced into Europe, specifically Sweden, in the 1960s. Stocks of indigenous crayfish had been dwindling due to the crayfish plague and it was hoped that the addition of this North American species would allow the considerable trade in crayfish to continue. What was not known at the time was that these imports were carriers of the same disease and likely to spread it further and faster. In 1976 they were introduced into the UK, much to the consternation of conservation groups who petitioned the Labour government about the threat to the indigenous species of crayfish. Much more notice should have been taken of these campaigners because after just five years it was clear the disease the new crayfish carried was having a detrimental impact on the native white-clawed species. But, by then, it was too late. As the Minister for Agriculture, Fisheries and Food stated in an answer to a question posed in 1986: 'Efforts now to eradicate crayfish plague would almost certainly be unsuccessful'. The continued existence of the native species is now very much in doubt.

Signal crayfish are also a threat to fish stocks, but not through disease. As omnivores, these predators, which closely resemble mini-lobsters and possess a level of aggression that far outstrips their size, eat anything, including fish spawn. They also breed in great numbers, spread rapidly, and are almost impossible to eliminate from even the smallest of lakes. Now that they have become established in the river systems of southern England, there is little doubt they will remain with us for the foreseeable future.

If young fish manage to evade the attentions of the signal crayfish and grow to a catchable size they then face an even greater threat: cormorants. Of the two sub-species of cormorant that inhabit Britain, it is the *sinensis* that causes the greatest damage to fish stocks.

Each winter vast numbers of these birds arrive from Northern Europe where they have been resident for many hundreds of years. Recent estimates suggest there may be as many as 60,000 birds over-wintering in Britain. If accurate, this suggests a rapidly increasing population both here and across Europe.

For those tasked with maintaining fish stocks, particularly in southern England, these birds present a significant problem because they are phenomenal predators. Such is their ability that in Asia and parts of Greece, they have been used to catch fish for human consumption for millennia. A snare is placed around the necks of trained birds which have been starved. These tethered birds are then released by the fisherman to catch whatever they can. Although they are able to swallow small fish, any larger specimens cannot pass the snare and can be extracted easily from the bird's throat by their owners. This type of fishing did make it to Western Europe in the 1500s; however by the late nineteenth century it was no longer practised in Britain.

The main threat these birds pose to fish stocks results from a combination of their increasing population and prodigious level of consumption. On average, a *sinensis* cormorant will eat over a pound of fish per day. Although this may seem minimal at first glance, once put in perspective, the impact of such predation becomes apparent.

The PAC recently introduced 250lbs of new fish into the Plough Pond. Within a couple of days, four cormorants were spotted. As the Club's Vice Chairman memorably remarked 'it was as if someone had sent them an email.' Eating just 1lb of fish per day, these four birds would consume all 3,500 of the new fish within two months. No lake can sustain such predation and on many fisheries it is even worse with the local cormorant population exceeding fifty birds. It is no surprise that angling clubs throughout the country see cormorants as a threat to their futures.

Should the fish evade both the crayfish and the cormorants and grow to a substantial size, they then have to ensure they do not end up in the claws of the otter. After a decline in numbers, the population of this carnivorous mammal was boosted in the 1980s and 1990s by the introduction of animals born in captivity. Otters are now having a detrimental effect on the fish stocks of the UK.

The impact of these apex predators is easily illustrated. The PAC introduced 103 carp into their lake late one November. More than 90 of these fish were into double figures, with the largest just shy of 20lbs. Over the following two winters an otter removed 18 of these fish; none weighed less than 10lbs at the time of capture, with the three largest fish in the lake killed, their stomachs eaten and the carcass left on the bank for the rats to enjoy. During this period the number of waterside birds also fell, again possibly due to the otter.

Of course, otter-proof fences can protect some venues. For many clubs though, this is simply not a viable option for several reasons. Financially, these fences are not cheap; many cost upwards of £20,000 which is well beyond the means of most clubs. For lakes sited on rented land the co-operation of the landowner needs to be sought, and given the unsightly nature of these barriers, they are far from likely to give permission for such structures to be erected on their property. Furthermore, some fisheries simply cannot be fenced. Lakes fed by streams pose particular problems, and it would be intriguing to learn how those who are keen to further increase the otter population would employ fencing to protect any of the nation's 1,500 rivers.

The Plough Pond could not be fenced. Even if it could it is doubtful the landowner would have allowed it, and the club certainly did not have the requisite funds to cover the cost when the otter first arrived. So it seemed that all the members could do was clean up the carcasses as the predator set about devouring the entire carp population. The outlook was depressing and at one point it was even suggested that the carp should be sold to another club. Moving the fish would have required health checks to prevent the unintended spread of disease, a perfectly reasonable policy. In order to undertake these checks, ten of the fish would have needed to be killed, something no club member was prepared to countenance. So the carp remained in the lake and at the mercy of the otter; and under prevailing legislation the club members' hands are tied.

Predation of fish stocks by otters is not new. Izaak Walton was fully aware of the issues caused by these predators, writing: 'I am sure the otter devours much fish, and kills and spoils much more than he eats.' Unfortunately, Walton was perfectly correct and photographic evidence from the PAC supports his claim. He did have a suggestion of how to prevent otter predation. Quoting Conrad Gessner, Walton advised the following: *'there is an herb, Benione, which being hung in a linen-cloth near a fish-pond, or any haunt that he uses, makes him to avoid the place'*. Benione, also known as 'Benjamin' or 'gum benzoin' is a resin extracted from the Styrax Benzoin tree found in Sumatra. It possesses a very strong scent that has been used in perfumes for many years. While I cannot comment on the veracity of this deterrent, an approach adopted slightly more recently does seem to be worth considering. In Victorian times, when expecting a visit from a member of the aristocracy or some other person of importance, several days before his arrival the riverkeepers would often hang lights from trees along the stretch of river their esteemed guest would be fishing. These lights would, it was thought, deter any otters. The PAC tried a similar approach using solar powered, rather than oil powered, lights and the results were surprising. Either the illuminations had an effect, or there was a remarkable coincidence, because while the lights were in place there were no further otter attacks. For clubs that are unable to otter-proof a lake, this may be an inexpensive alternative worth pursuing.

When fishing the Thames, the question I get asked most often is 'Do you eat the fish?' I always reply in the negative and many of the questioners are surprised and tend to respond with 'So why do you catch them?' Of course, humans have used the rivers, canals and lakes of the country as a food source for thousands of years. It is only relatively recently that fishing for pleasure has become more commonplace than fishing for food. My father, who was never an angler, caught fish as a child during the war years of the 1940s simply to provide food for his family. Strangely, whenever I talk to him about a particular fish I have caught, he'll respond with a reference to how tasty they are, or how difficult they can be to scale. Eating coarse fish was often depicted on film. In the Ealing Studios wonderful comedy *Passport to Pimlico* which was set in the post war years of food shortages and rationing, the fish-obsessed fishmonger Frank Huggins (played by John Slater) is seen selling a customer a dead bronze bream of around 3lbs.

The angling writers of earlier times invariably mentioned dressing and eating fish in their books. Izaak Walton's *The Compleat Angler* is littered with examples of how fish should be prepared for the table. For both carp and chub, Walton expends a great many words detailing not just his favoured method of cooking but also how to flavour them and which herbs and spices should be used. Keeping fish fresh was not as easy in the 17th century as it is now. Sir John Hawkins claimed that carp live longest out of water, and that in the Netherlands he had witnessed these fish to be kept alive 'for three or four weeks, by hanging them up in a net, in a cool place, surrounded by wet moss, and feeding them with bread and milk.' This is difficult to accept in two key respects. First, that carp would survive without water for so long, and second, why would anyone subject a fish to such treatment when superior methods of preserving the meat for human consumption were available?

An alternative way to maintain a fresh stock of fish was to create a stew pond. These had been in use since the medieval era and were commonly found in the grounds of monasteries and the stately homes of the aristocracy. At Newstead Abbey near Nottingham, the monks created an impressive stew pond for retaining carp which still remains open to visitors, but not anglers, over 500 years after its construction. For anyone wanting to fish one of these historic venues, the stew pond near Epsom is an option since it is open for fishing on a day ticket basis.

Fish farming in this manner was not restricted to Britain. Across Europe, fish were retained in ponds as a source of food, even in those countries where the winters are much colder than in England and ponds of considerable depth are prone to freezing. While the species of fish that were farmed varied from nation to nation, in France and Poland the bream was held in high esteem. Izaak Walton references this and quotes the following French proverb: *'He that hath breams in his pond is able to bid his friend welcome.'* Walton adds that the tastiest parts of the bream are the belly and head. Personally I'd rather see them swim away unharmed than even contemplate eating the head of this wonderful fish. The BBC, disappointingly, seems to be less discerning. On the food section of its website there are recipes for both perch and pike, the latter being a species that appears to be in decline.

Despite the access to fresh fish, either from stew ponds or the waterways of the nation, it is contended that up to half of all the fish eaten were preserved in some way. Of the others only a relatively small fraction were fresh coarse fish, the bulk being saltwater fish, although this varied by location. By way of example, the kitchens of Westminster Abbey had access to both coarse and sea fish, and served a range of species throughout the year. In terms of coarse fish, roach and dace were served regularly during the winter months with most of these taken from the Thames. On festival days the monks enjoyed pike (with cinnamon and ginger sauce) and salmon. These were fish caught in the river with the monks exercising their right to a tithe on all such fish landed from specific stretches.

Naturally, the removal of fish reduces the overall level of fish stocks. For this reason many angling clubs introduced size limits. These guidelines were designed to allow fish to breed before they could be taken for the table, thus expanding the fish population. Although many 21st century angling clubs do not allow their members to kill fish, the taking of fish for food is still permitted by law. Strict rules govern how many fish can be kept. At present, only one pike can be taken from a river each day and it must be no longer than 65cm. However, two grayling may be killed for food providing they are between 30cm and 38cm, and up to fifteen other fish up to 20cm including barbel, chub, bronze bream, common carp, crucian carp, dace, perch, rudd, silver bream, roach, smelt and tench. Interestingly these rules stipulate upper size limits (8 inches in the case of the smaller fish); historically size limits were all minima. For instance, in the Victorian era, no chub under 9 inches could be killed for food, nor roach and perch under 8 inches; dace and smelts had to be at least 6 inches before they could legally be taken, gudgeon 5 inches; and pike and barbel had to exceed 12 inches. All measurements were taken from the eye of the fish to the fork in the tail, and anyone found to have killed undersized fish was subject to a fine of £5 for each offence, equivalent to 15 days' work for a skilled tradesman. Though rules of this fashion can be applied to the predation of fish by humans, it is not easy to limit the catch of other predators. Telling an otter to take no more than three double-figure carp per month has little impact.

The level of predation by birds and animals appears to have increased significantly in recent years, and it is difficult to see how this will change unless there is intervention. No administration would sanction the culling of otters or cormorants to preserve fish stocks simply because fish are, in the main, invisible to the general public. Whether the river they are walking by holds any fish or not, is not something of which most people are aware or even consider.

Non-anglers do not see the impact of predation. While many of them might spot an otter and think 'how lovely', they are oblivious to the damage these apex predators do beneath the surface of the water. Without change, the result will probably be even less river and canal fishing, and more angling behind high wire fences that give the venues the appearance of compounds from a bygone era which were designed to keep prisoners in, rather than predators out.

CHAPTER 9

BLAME IT
ON THE BOOGIE

Canal fishing in sub-zero temperatures;
broken poles; bankside serenading;
and gudgeon.

Opening the car door the chill morning air takes me by surprise, it's definitely colder than when I left home 35 minutes ago. Rather than recoiling into the vehicle to enjoy the warmth, probably the wisest thing to do, I tentatively venture out and slowly pull my boots on while briefly contemplating the chances of catching fish from a frigid, crystal clear canal in mid-winter. I conclude they are slim at best. Today we're at Kintbury, a small village located a few miles east of Hungerford on the banks of the Kennet and Avon Canal and it's far too early for any sensible person to be out of their bed.

The angler in the adjacent car looks my way: 'Gonna be a Diana Ross day,' he says in a manner that's annoyingly upbeat for such an early hour.

'What?' I reply.

'Diana Ross day.' He pauses for a second or two for dramatic effect, then adds 'Three degrees,' with a superfluous slice of cheerfulness that the comment did not entirely warrant.

'Sorry, too early for such subtlety, I'm still half asleep,' I murmur.

'I've been up since five, never can sleep on the night before a match,' he complains. At least I'm not the only one with that problem.

'But Diana Ross wasn't in the…' before I could finish, with his kit loaded on to a barrow my fellow angler strolls off to find the Match Secretary and is immediately replaced by Gary.

'Don't you own a coat,' he says from within a t-shirt, a fleece, a hoodie, a coat, and some form of head covering that more closely resembles a balaclava than a fishing hat.

'If you go to the building society, Gary, make sure you leave that at home,' is the best I can come up with by way of a rejoinder.

'Yes, I could get arrested I suppose, but masks are in at the moment, aren't they?'

'Not that sort.'

He laughs, 'I just don't get it, do you ever feel the cold?'

'Now and then, but not often,' is my truthful reply. For some reason, as I have grown older I have become less affected by cold weather. I will often fish in a t-shirt while the others are in fleeces, and will sometimes overheat in a fleece when my companions are snugly wrapped in heavy coats. The heat of summer is another matter though. Once the temperature climbs above the early twenties centigrade I find it far too hot. Tiredness rapidly seeps into every part of my body and within a short time I feel utterly exhausted and distinctly unwell. Give me a Diana Ross day times five as my angling companion might say (even though Ross was in *The Supremes*, not *The Three Degrees*), or 15 degrees in more conventional meteorological terminology, and I'd be more than happy.

There is one exception to this rule though: my feet. Before the creation of thermal boots (the finest fishing-related invention of all time) I would wear two pairs of socks when fishing. It didn't help much and made getting my wellingtons on more difficult. Soon after arriving at the bank I would feel my feet begin to cool, even though my body remained warm. A couple of hours later, that coolness would become uncomfortable, and not long after I'd have to pack up simply due to the pain induced by the cold weather. Walking would then be difficult because my feet were so painful. Invariably it felt as if I had clods of clay, or some other type of mud, stuck to the underside of my boots. At home a shower would help, but even bare footed I could still feel the hard lumps pressing into the soles of my feet, an impediment that would remain until I had fully rewarmed.

Quite why this happened I have never been able to determine, but I expect there is a simple medical answer which has so far eluded me, possibly 'cold feet syndrome' or something more exotic-sounding when expressed in Latin, as many illnesses are, such as *pedum frigidorum signa*. How the Victorian match anglers managed to stave off the cold remains a mystery, and as for those Arctic Explorers of the same period, I can only applaud their fortitude when faced with week after week of sub-zero temperatures.

While it may not be ten below, today is unquestionably cold. Low overnight temperatures have fixed all existing wheel ruts into a semi-permanent state and the frosted earth is clinging to the soles of our boots more assuredly than damp groundbait grips a method feeder, to paraphrase Ted Hughes.

'Ok Gary, I'll get a coat!'

'Good, we don't want you falling in due to hypothermia. It would spoil the fishing.'

A short while ago the draw gave me peg 2: a reasonable peg and almost the shortest walk. The Match Secretary, wearing one of his pointier hats, is to my right on peg 1 (the end peg again), and the Club's Vice Chairman is to my left on peg 3. Being sandwiched between two excellent canal anglers reduces my chance of winning, but with these two either side of me it will certainly make the day more entertaining.

Depending on the water level in the river Kennet, the canal's current can vary considerably in this section from almost non-existent to a raging torrent. Today it is slow, which will allow me to use a 0.2g float on each of my three rigs: one for fishing maggots, one for pinkies (the larvae of green bottle flies which are much smaller than maggots), and another for worms. A boat is moored in front of me, ideal ambush territory for a perch, so I'll feed that area with worms and hope to catch a bonus fish or two. The bulk of my weight should come from roach and maybe a few skimmers (small bream) which I hope to catch 'down the track' (i.e. the middle of the canal).

With ten minutes to the whistle, the clouds are definitely looking darker than they were half an hour ago; we could be in for some rain later. My rigs are ready to go, the bait is prepared, and I have compacted my kit into the smallest possible area to give walkers and bikers as much room to pass as possible, so it is time for a pre-match coffee while I listen to a woodpecker hammering on a tree at a tempo that even the most talented drummer could not hope to replicate.

'Come on Danny, blow the whistle it'll be getting dark soon,' an angler calls from along the bank. I've just filled my baiting cup with chopped worms and turn to the Match Secretary. He has his mobile phone in hand and is leaning forward, looking along the line of anglers all keen to get started like sprinters in a 100m final. He glances back to the phone, back to the anglers, back to his phone. Each time he does that, he rocks back and forth a little on his seatbox. The whistle is between his lips virtually hidden by his beard which is much bushier and whiter than usual. Any second now he'll start the match, at least he should. Beyond him a couple of middle-aged walkers are coming our way, 'Hurry up Danny, I want to get the pole shipped out before they get to me,' I say to myself. Danny's focus is now entirely on his phone as he watches the seconds tick towards 9:00.

The shrill tone of the whistle breaks the calm and the tension, and I start to ship out the worms. But an even louder, unexpected noise stops me abruptly: a thunderous splash from my right. A pair of mallards, startled by the sound, flap and skate as quickly as they can across the surface of the water, clearly fearing for their lives. Something has happened and I am not quite sure what until I turn to look upstream. I was half expecting to see one of the walkers climbing out of the canal, but they were both still warm and dry and walking in my direction. What greets my eyes is a scene that instantly makes sense of the hubbub. At the moment Danny blew the whistle the bank under his seatbox collapsed. He is now sat in the Kennet and Avon Canal, a look of bewilderment on his face, phone firmly gripped in his left hand, and the whistle still between his lips. My pole is only half shipped out, so before I offer any assistance I need to get the worms over to the boat otherwise they will be lost mid channel. I also need to stop laughing.

'You okay?' I call as I begin to retract the pole.

'Bank collapsed.'

'I know, I can see that. Do you need any help?' I reply. Danny is now scrambling out of the water; fortunately the canal is shallow in the margins, but it's still deep enough to get him wet and today is not a good day to be sitting in wet clothes.

'Are you wet?' I continue.

'No, just my feet, it got into my boots, rest of me is dry.'

The two walkers didn't break stride or crack a smile. But as they pass behind me, the man turns to his female companion, his face deadpan without the slightest flicker of emotion, 'That reminds me,' he says, 'I need to get that gnome out of the pond when we get back.'

Thirty minutes into the match and Danny is finally fishing. I've made a decent start with a few roach in the net, but it has just begun to snow. It was quite light at first, now it's much heavier and I'll have to set up the umbrella. Without a connector to attach the brolly to my seatbox, I have to ensure it is firmly rooted into the ground. On most venues that's not an issue, the towpath of the canal though is very stony and getting the support deep enough is not easy – especially when I would rather be catching fish.

With the umbrella in place, I am at least protected, more importantly so too is my bait. The snow does collect on the pole, though, making my hands wet each time I ship it in and out. It's time to try over by the boat, where hopefully a few large perch are enjoying the worms I potted in earlier. Reaching for the perch rig, my shoulder rubs against the umbrella support. The upright twists gently, then, before I can grab it, the whole structure falls. This would not have been a problem had it fallen in any other direction. However it fell precisely across my pole which, being supported by two rollers, is at its most vulnerable. The weight of the brolly crushes the carbon rendering the number 4 section unusable. With no spare section with me, I am now reduced to fishing just a top three for the remainder of the match, restricting the distance I can reach to a mere 3.9m. The perch by the boat will have to wait for another day.

Breaking such a critical pole section means there's very little chance of me winning this contest. All I can do is bait a swim much closer to the bank and hope to draw the roach from further out to where I can reach and then catch a great many small fish very quickly.

Two hours into the match and Nick on peg 3 has just banked a decent perch from his long pole line. Fortunately I am catching fish using just the top three pole sections, but they are small, and mostly gudgeon. Danny is also catching well, plenty of nice roach, and at this stage he is probably in front. He has also just fed some worms on the long pole line hoping for the same result as Nick.

There is just an hour to go now. I'm still catching, but no larger fish have moved in, so I am stuck with a seemingly inexhaustible shoal of gudgeon. Fortunately my catch rate has improved due to the fact that it has stopped snowing and the pole-breaking umbrella is lying on the ground. Without the canvas overhead, I can more easily lift the fish to hand which speeds up the process of getting them from canal and into the keepnet. Nick's catch rate has slowed slightly, but his fish are of a better stamp, and Danny now has a very big perch in his net. I have not heard a great deal from the other anglers, maybe they are catching so fast there's no time to talk, hopefully they are struggling in which case I might have a chance of making the first three.

Yet more commotion to my right. Danny is still on his seatbox, which is a relief, but there's definitely the sound of voices and fibreglass scraping on concrete. Looking beyond the Match Secretary I can see two young women, possibly mid-twenties, launching a canoe. One has climbed in, and the other is passing her various items including, what looks like, a black plastic cuboid of about eight inches across its longest dimension. What can it be? Both are in the boat now and are arranging their oars. One reaches for the cuboid and now I know what it is. Although I cannot see it anymore, I can hear it: the mysterious box is some type of sound system. A very loud sound system would be a better description. The strains of an electric guitar, energised by BB King or Eric Clapton, floating musically over the rippling canal would have been greatly appreciated, by me at least. But rowing to a Blues beat would be too slow for these two accomplished oarswomen. Something much more up tempo was their choice and the unmistakable sound of *The Jackson 5* is echoing along the waterway: 'My baby's always dancin'.

As the canoe nears Danny I can see from his rather gruff expression that he is not a 'Jacksons' fan but he keeps his thoughts to himself. Already Michael is into the first rendition of the chorus. With the craft making its way past peg 1, the volume increases and the fish in my swim get to feel the vibrations from 'Don't blame it on the moonlight' which, for some inexplicable reason, I hum to myself. 'Don't blame it on the good times' is the parting shot as the canoe, now travelling at a decent rate, glides past me. Then, as it reaches Nick, a chorus of several voices from the bank, in perfect time, but not quite perfect pitch, chant in unison like a football crowd: 'Blame it on the boogie'. I can see the rowers smiling in appreciation at the club's vocal efforts. Thankfully no one requests an encore.

Fortunately the intervention of a little disco fever did not affect the fishing. Danny had a much better last hour than first hour, and I managed to bank a few more tiny gudgeon. At the weigh-in we initially thought Danny had won, which would have been just compensation for his earlier mishap.

'Look at the belly on that,' someone behind me called out.

'He's not as fat as you,' was the swift reply from another angler.

'I meant the net.'

Danny's net did indeed have quite a belly to it caused by the roach and perch which in total weighed over 8lbs, a good weight for this stretch of the canal at this time of year. It was eclipsed by Leslie's 15lbs of bream, though. My 176 fish, mostly gudgeon, were nowhere near enough to get me a payout.

With the cost of travel, bait, pools money, and of course a new number 4 section, today was particularly expensive for me. Yet even with these additional costs, the snow, and my inadequate weight of fish, this match has to be one of the most memorable I have fished recently. Fishing alongside good friends, whether it is in a match or not, always improves the day, and even if the fishing is not quite as good as hoped, these are days that, when entered into life's diary, are always accompanied by a smile.

While my weight of gudgeon did not get me any financial reward in the match, they still kept me entertained. Despite being one of the mini species, this tough little fish is held in great affection by many anglers. Some of the most esteemed angling writers devote whole chapters about *gobio gobio*, while others pen essays detailing their admiration for this diminutive fish. It is difficult to be certain why this is the case, but one reason may be that the gudgeon is above all an *honest* fish. If an angler puts any bait of an acceptable size near a gudgeon, then it will be eaten. Although worms have always been thought to be their preferred food, gudgeon do not seem to be at all fussy.

I distinctly remember fishing a tributary of the Thames for roach a few years ago using sweetcorn to avoid the bleak. The float kept disappearing and I kept striking without success. Time after time I missed the fish, and believing them to be quality roach I was not in a particularly good humour. Finally I connected with one; but it was not a roach, instead it was a very big gudgeon. Then another came to hand, and then another. Although I was disappointed that I had not landed a netful of highly prized specimen red fins, I had to smile at the sheer tenacity of these greedy little fish that had kept me enthralled for so long. Gudgeon also seem less affected by the weather, feeding when most other fish are hiding away. Once hooked, they invariably fight as hard as they can. Unlike some fish, a gudgeon does not take the easy way out of the very one-sided battle by rolling onto its side and allowing the angler to land it without effort. It fights all the way in, for which it has to be admired.

These qualities have resulted in some anglers becoming spellbound by them, eschewing all other species just to focus for long periods of their angling lives on gudgeon. This is not a modern day phenomenon driven by some influential social media users; it's a peculiar fascination that has been a part of coarse fishing for many years. Writing in the mid-1800s, Edward Jesse acknowledged the allure of gudgeon fishing, noting that it was not uncommon to see three or four anglers fishing for gudgeon from a single punt on the Thames, 'watching a float as it glides down the stream before them, the sun sometimes scorching them, and at others the rain wetting them through.' I'm not sure Edward Jesse was quite so enamoured with the gudgeon, but he did know of others who were, adding that 'the clergyman of a parish in the neighbourhood of Hampton Court, who was engaged to be married to the daughter of a bishop, enjoyed his gudgeon fishing so much that he arrived too late to be married, and the lady, offended at his neglect, refused to be united.'

Perhaps the good vicar was after one of the monster-sized gudgeon reputedly found in the Thames at the time. These mythological fish were reported to be in excess of ten inches in length and weighing over a pound. Given that he was undoubtedly of virtuous character, he would no doubt have accepted such tales as truthful, whereas they were more likely either wild exaggerations or possibly misidentifications. A gudgeon exceeding four ounces would be a remarkable capture, so I am confident that one of over sixteen ounces has never existed in the river Thames or any other waterway of Great Britain.

Not only was the gudgeon sought for the sport it provided, the Victorians also prized this little fish for its taste and medicinal qualities. One author of the era asserted that there is no Thames fish more palatable than gudgeon '*fried with a plentiful supply of lard*'. Another noted that '*in a gastronomic point of view, the gudgeon gives precedence to none: a fry of fat gudgeon, eaten piping hot, with a squeeze of lemon juice, is a dish to set before a king.*' In his view the gudgeon were superior to other fish as '*Moet's champagne is to gooseberry pop.*' Having never tasted gudgeon, nor 'gooseberry pop', I cannot attest to the accuracy of this statement, though it should be remembered that this was a time when calf ear fritters, beef and lark pie, sheep trotters (skinned and boiled), and spinach ice-cream were normal fayre. Fortunately our tastes have changed in the intervening years.

With regard to their healing qualities, consuming gudgeon was considered to be an excellent way of 'increasing good blood'. Writing about 100 years earlier than the Victorian food critics, the author of *Angling Improved* was adamant that gudgeon could be used to combat a range of illnesses. His opinion was that the humble gudgeon '*are of great Vertue against the Cholick arising from cold, and tarterous Humours; broil'd and eaten without Salt, are good against the Bloody-Flux, and other Fluxes of the Belly.*' Furthermore it was not necessary to consume the fish to profit from its magical medicinal properties (though swallowing them whole and alive was a preferred approach). Applying the fish to wounds resulting from the *'Bitings of Mad-dogs and Serpents'* would bring almost instant relief to the sufferer. Anyone unlucky enough to be bitten by a mad dog while simultaneously suffering from a stomach complaint, but lucky enough to be holding a gudgeon, could quickly apply the fish to the external wound before eating it. Personally I would prefer to opt for an antiseptic cream and glass of Coca Cola. The medicinal qualities of this remarkable fish did not end with the healing of bites and stomach disorders; apparently those poisoned by *Dorycinum* (a common poisonous plant) would also benefit from the application of a gudgeon.

Based on this evidence, it is easy to see why gudgeon were held in such esteem by our fishing ancestors. For the match anglers of today, they can be a nuisance, but they can also turn a bad day into a good one. For that alone, the gudgeon is a fish for which I have much affection.

CHAPTER 10

AN EXCEPTIONAL DAY

More match practise; parking issues;
a netful of roach; fishing for life.

As usual sleep is elusive on the night before a match, so I'm wide awake. It's a little past 4am on the first Sunday in December and I can hear the distant drone of vehicles on the main road. Where are they going at such an early hour? Even Bicester Village shopping centre doesn't open this early. Or maybe it does in December.

In what seems like only a handful of seconds later, but in reality is almost two hours, my alarm clock screams into action. I slip silently out of bed, as always, but it's to no avail: Sara is already awake.

'We need to get you a new alarm clock.'

'Why? That one has served me well for over forty years,' is my somewhat too hasty reply. I should have given it a little more thought.

'It's too loud; too aggressive for this time of day,' is the rather abrupt response.

'How would you like me to wake you then? Using aroma therapy perhaps? Maybe I should gently waft the scent of a fried breakfast under your nose.' Will I never learn? There's a time and a place for attempts at humour and 6am on a Sunday quite clearly isn't it.

'I'd prefer it if you didn't wake me at all,' is the sternest of replies. The conversation has the feeling that it has ended, so I collect my clothes and head out of the bedroom. It's then I hear 'Good luck!'

Washed, dressed, sandwiches and coffee made, maggots and worms out of the fridge and in my bait bag – finally I'm ready to leave. There's only one problem: my hair is all over the place. Normally some liberally applied water is sufficient to organise it into some satisfactory arrangement. Not today though. It was only recently cut and clumps of it need to be turned a full 180°. Water just isn't powerful enough. I could go as I am, but if I win or catch a big chub there will be photos and I never come out well in photographs as it is, so with hair like this they would look even more disturbing. I could go back into the bedroom and grab a pot of hair gel. I've done it before and to be honest it has never worked out well, so there's only one option: a woolly hat. Hats tend to make my face look even fatter than it does already, but today's forecast is for a sharp frost, followed by a north easterly wind, so a hat is probably advisable in any case. Now I can leave.

But something is stopping me. Somewhere in the back of my mind a voice is telling me I have forgotten something.

Unfortunately this particularly unhelpful 'voice' refuses to tell me exactly what I have left behind. One more check in the garage then I'm on the road, with or without whatever it is.

Christmas lights are glittering on almost every house as I drive through the village. Although they make an impressive display I'm not sure who benefits from these light shows so early on a cold, dark, Sunday morning.

Getting out of the car I can hear the low mumble of voices coming from the anglers readying themselves for what could be a difficult day. Many are wearing headtorches, including the Match Secretary who has already walked along the river ensuring the pegs he intends to use are fishable. In the distance an owl acknowledges the dawn with a mournful call. A magpie shrieks his tuneless response: a wake-up call to his slumbering brethren. The magpie is making it clear that now is the time to feed; the owl, having fed through the night, is signalling that it is time to sleep – that feels like a really good idea.

Even with twenty-five minutes to draw time, I'm still the last to arrive, which is yet again noted by Danny.

'What's with the hat? Unusual to see you in a hat,' he asks after telling me I'm late arriving – again.

'Oh, just a bad hair day,' is my honest reply. He shrugs his shoulders, 'You know this is a fishing match not a fashion shoot?' he adds.

'Nor is it fancy dress,' I reply while pointing to the red hat with a white pom-pom he is wearing.

'It's Christmas!' he replies grinning. One man does not need that many hats.

'Anyway, I hear you were practising down here the other day,' he continues.

'Maybe.'

'Bill told me you were.'

'How did he know?'

'Les told him.'

'How did…does everyone know?'

'Probably, you can't keep secrets in this club, you know.'

In that respect he is perfectly correct. Even without recourse to social media, very little fishing-related information goes unnoticed, especially amongst the match anglers.

'You not going to tell me how you got on then?'

'Course I will Danny,' I say smiling, 'after the match'. He looks none too pleased.

'Give us your pools money then, it's only a fiver because it's Christmas.'

After examining previous Christmas Match results, I realised that it was more often than not won by an angler who caught chub. Historically, not many fish have been caught in this event, with a single four-pounder enough to scoop the prize. Given that I am more of a small fish angler, I thought it prudent to have a pre-match practise alongside someone with a good track record at catching such fish. Phil, a good friend of mine, is a big-fish angler. He would much rather catch a single 25lbs carp than a dozen 6oz roach, something I find difficult to comprehend. Phil jumped at the chance of a day's chubbing, so last Sunday we piled our gear into the back of his little white van and made our way to the river with the intention of fishing until a little after dark.

The parking arrangements for river anglers are different in the winter when the ground has been softened by rain.

Rather than park in the field adjacent to the Thames, we are required to leave our vehicles along a long tarmac track, with two wheels on the grass and two on the track to prevent getting stuck and at the same time leaving adequate space for others to pass. As we turned off the main road and crossed the cattle grid that provides access to the farm track, we could see an old, green, muddy, Vauxhall Astra. Apparently Danny was also practising.

'Bet he's on peg 2,' Phil said.

'Bound to be.'

We turned around at the end of the track and made our way back to his car.

'I've got an idea, Phil. Why don't we park really tight to his bumper.'

'Why?'

'He'll pack up before us, and when he gets to his car he'll have to put his kit down, get in the car, start the engine and pull forward before he can load his gear away. He'll be furious, especially with so much space for us to park in.'

Phil and Danny have fished together since they were teenagers so they're good friends and get on well. Danny would know there's no malice in our practical joke, but he would, all the same, be very annoyed. Just what we were after.

I climbed out and assisted Phil as he drew the van closer and closer to the Astra's bumper. Waving him forward, inch by inch, we finally stopped when the gap was less than a hand's width. Perfect.

As we climbed the stile that leads into the field through which the river flows we were still laughing at the thought of his reaction. Of course, we would not be there to witness his dismay and utter incredulity that someone would be so foolish as to park in that manner. It was easy, though, to imagine how he would react. In fact we would probably hear him as we fished from over 500 yards away!

In the distance we could see a green umbrella positioned as protection from the wind on peg 2 so we made our way over for a chat. As we neared the umbrella, I said, while feebly trying to disguise my voice: 'Can I see your permit?'

'Course, mate,' came the reply in an accent I did not recognise. With that, the angler stood up and came around to our side of the brolly. Neither Phil nor I are exceptionally tall, about average height, and our new acquaintance towered over us. 'There you go,' he added.

'Thanks,' I replied in my usual voice and a little taken aback, 'any luck?'

We chatted for a while then I mentioned that another fishing colleague was somewhere along the bank.

'Not seen anyone else, mate,' he said, 'and I've been here since first light.'

'Well, he must be at the other end, we know he's here because we're parked next to him.'

'The green Astra?'

'Yes.'

'That's my car,' the giant replied.

A tentative 'Oh' was all I could muster as the potential consequences of our childish actions began to take shape. Our new angling compatriot did not look like the type of person who would appreciate being the victim of a practical joke, especially one perpetrated by two people he didn't know. Phil was avidly watching the angler's quiver tip in case he had a knock, and not really paying attention.

'Phil, that's not Danny's car then.'

'What?'

'The Astra belongs to this man.'

'Oh, right,' he replied looking back towards the rod.

I just stared at him, urging him to connect the dots. This is when it would be helpful if telepathy was real. I cleared my throat, Phil looked at me, and I stared back in earnest. The instant of realisation on Phil's face was magical, his eyes widened and he swallowed deeply.

'I think I've left something in the van,' he mumbled, 'won't be a minute.'

'If I have what you've forgotten, you can borrow it.'

It was a kind gesture from the fisherman. 'If only you knew what we know,' I thought.

'It's fine, best of luck,' Phil replied and made off across the field in some haste without looking back.

Collecting all the tackle together I too wished the angler good luck and made my way along the bank recounting what a close call that was. When Phil returned, we dissolved into laughter. 'He wouldn't have minded,' Phil asserted, 'he could have picked the van up in one hand and moved it if he needed to.'

After that stuttering start, the practise session went well – at least it did for Phil: I blanked but he had a 5lbs chub, a wonderful fish with an unusual black spot on her cheek. My failure to connect with the intended quarry was not too surprising, though it did leave me in a bit of a quandary about how to approach the match. In the end I decided to make my decision at the peg, after all the river changes from day to day, so conditions could be very different come match day.

Earlier this morning the draw gave me peg 17. As I look across the swim it appears completely featureless. A few short months ago there would have been a fish-holding willow tree I could cast to. Not now, and not for any time soon. The main flow looks faster than it did on practise day, so I have decided to opt for two lines: a stick float along the crease nearest to me, and a cage feeder approach for a line near to the far bank, providing I can get it to hold in place.

The slate grey sky looks a little ominous, we could get rain later; hopefully it will be delayed until after the final whistle. Failing to catch, and getting saturated, would not make for a good day.

The nagging voice in the back of my mind has not given up and all the while I was tackling up I was expecting to find out what it is I have forgotten. But my rods and reels were safely packed, along with a tackle box of bits and pieces, two tubes of floats, hook lengths, feeders, bait dropper and catapults. Nothing appears to be missing, so why do I have this uncomfortable feeling?

There's still fifteen minutes to go before we start, so plenty of time for a coffee, a sausage roll, and to refresh my groundbait. The sausage roll cannot be healthy because it tastes so good; the coffee is on the cool side, maybe it's time to get a new flask; as for the groundbait, well that's reminded me of what I have forgotten.

Over the last few years I seem to have developed an allergy to groundbait. Not ideal for a coarse angler. Whether the allergy has been caused by changes in my physiology, or a new component added to the groundbait mix, I am not sure. Regrettably the ingredients are not printed on bags of groundbait, which does seem strange with so many people now allergic to various foodstuffs, so I cannot isolate what causes me to sneeze uncontrollable for hours on end after even just smelling the bait. The solution is for me to take an anti-histamine tablet before fishing; today I forgot.

I've balled some groundbait in where I intend to fish the stick float and have just put the feeder out. As I cast it out I am not entirely sure it would hold in the current. And I'll have to wait until the next cast to find out because the tip has started shaking and pulling round already – fish on. One cast and I have a roach in the net, not the start I expected, but one I very much welcome. The roach tend to pack together at this time of year as protection from predators, maybe there's a huge shoal in front of me – I can only hope there is.

Two hours in and while the rate at which the fish have come to my net has dramatically slowed, the rate at which I am sneezing has dramatically increased. My groundbait allergy is really kicking in, making my eyes stream so much that I can hardly see the rod tip. After another hour, or maybe two, it should ease but until then it'll be a little like fishing in the dark.

Well into the last hour now and the fish have pretty much left my swim; at least my sneezing is not quite as frequent as earlier and my eyes, though sore and stinging, are not permanently filled with tears. I've been lucky so far with a few roach and dace, but reports are coming back that Steve on the upstream end peg has had an excellent day; Leslie on the next peg down from him is catching at a good rate too. Both are excellent river anglers, so it's not that surprising.

Steve has reached legendary status in the PAC for his angling exploits. A watchmaker by trade, he brings a degree of precision to his angling that no other club member can match. His hand-tied hooklengths, of which he normally has around 150, are as good, if not better, than any shop-bought equivalents; the shot on his pole rigs are always perfectly arranged to suit the conditions; and his line never displays any of the kinks or suspicious-looking imperfections that most of us are quite prepared to tolerate. This level of attention to detail was a key factor in his success in the 200-peg Upper

Thames Championship as well as helping him to fifth place in the 100-peg section in the Division 3 National.

Steve has fished most of his life. For his eighth Christmas he received a bamboo cane rod, with rings held on by red tape, which was paired with a centre pin-type reel. The following day he was fishing a local lake with a flour and water paste for bait; Steve had already fallen under angling's magic spell that draws so many of us from the comfort of our homes to the banks of the rivers and lakes day after day.

Little did he know in those early days that there would be a time in his life when fishing was no longer an option. In the early 1990s, Steve received the type of news that no one wants to hear: he was diagnosed with leukaemia. Within a short space of time, Steve's body was so ravaged by the cancer that he was physically unable to fish and in his darkest moments thought that he would never again see the float tip disappear or the quiver tip shake then bend in that fashion that stirs the soul of even the most hardened angler. But he was not going to give in easily. With treatment, support from his family and friends, no little willpower, and extraordinary strength of character, Steve was, eventually, able to get back to the sport he loves so much. Thirty years on from that fateful day when the devastating ailment was first diagnosed, Steve is fishing as well as he ever has.

The final whistle has sounded. Although I have caught enough to win an average Christmas Match, the river has fished exceptionally well today with, according to reports, some pegs producing notable weights of roach. I can see Danny making his way along the bank, the white pom-pom on his Christmas hat bobbing, as a bobble should, in time with his stride.

'Come on then, let's get this done,' he says with his usual lack of warmth. I offered to help with the weigh-in today, so with clipboard in hand I join him and we make our way to the end peg. As he cleans his kit, Leslie confirms that he's done well. This, of course, is just phase one of the big clean, at home with access to a power washer and washing machine (for the nets) Leslie will undertake phase two. Strangely he does not offer to do mine as well.

Steve looks very pleased and admits to having an excellent day with plenty of roach and dace. As he lifts the net, ring by ring, the splashing begins. The shorter the net becomes the greater is the level of commotion – he has indeed had an exceptional day. With the fish now on the bank there's an opportunity to see one of the best bags of roach ever taken in a match along this stretch of the Thames. The weak winter sun reflects off the thousands of scales, producing an array of colours that more than matches any rainbow. It's a splendid sight, I only wish I had put those fish in the net and not Steve. Danny hooks the spring balance to the weigh sling and the dial immediately spins round. As the fish stop jumping he reads out the weight and I make a note on the match sheet: 19lbs 3oz. It's a stunning weight for this time of year, and at least we now know where all the roach can be found.

Leslie has also caught well today. His netful of roach weighed just over 10lbs, easily putting him in second place. Unfortunately I did not make the frame, though I did enjoy the day. Normally the December matches are slow days with very little caught. At least I had the enjoyment of catching more than I thought I would, but where are the chub? I originally thought chub would be the key to winning this match but not a single one was landed. I suppose that's all part of the glorious uncertainty of river fishing.

As I made my way back to the car, I noticed a young child of about four or five years old paddling in the shallow margins, his protective parents looking on. It is often remarked that the olfactory sense is the strongest for awakening memories, but in this case the stimulus was visual. His splashing around in wellingtons triggered a memory that had lain dormant for many years, and yet rather surprisingly was particularly vivid: the day I caught fish for the very first time. As to its exact level of accuracy I cannot attest. Often such memories are, in intervening years, overlaid with idealisations of what actually happened. Places and people may have been stored safely and remain unaffected by time, but events will inevitably become less precise as they fall deeper into history. Notwithstanding those reservations this is my current recollection of that first day by the river.

As a young child I spent every weekend and a substantial part of my school holidays with my grandparents who lived a few miles away in Abingdon. For as long as anyone at that time could remember, Abingdon had been synonymous with fishing. The town which Charles Dickens rather unkindly referred to in his *Dictionary of the Thames* as 'quiet even to the point of dulness', is dominated by waterways. The river Ock flows through the centre of Abingdon on its way to meeting the Thames, and from 1810 the Wilts and Berks Canal provided a vital link between the West Country and the Midlands. This waterway in particular played a significant role in the development of Abingdon's economy throughout the Victorian era. Although abandoned in 1914, it is gratifying to learn that the canal is currently undergoing a restoration and could, in a few years' time, once again link the Thames to the Kennet and Avon Canal.

My grandfather worked in the building industry all of his life. He was a roofer by trade, but turned his hand to most building-related tasks when employed by Abingdon Town Council (later Vale Of The White Horse District Council). As part of the maintenance team, he was required to repair, to the best of his ability, any issue that may have arisen with the council-owned properties, usually the houses that were rented to local residents. Not overly tall, his skin was bronzed by the countless hours spent on slate and tile roofs, as well as the six years he toured around the Middle East, North Africa, Italy and finally Germany as a Gunner in the Royal Artillery in the early 1940s. This period was possibly the only time in his adult life when he was seen outside without his customary brown trilby that concealed his Brylcreemed, jet-black hair. He was a fisherman, vegetable gardener, keeper of pigs and chicken, and a practical joker, especially where his five brothers were concerned. Fishing was his main pastime. He fished whenever he had the opportunity, teaching his daughter, my mother, how to fish. Even now, on occasions when I have performed well-below par in a match, my mother will claim with utter conviction that she 'would have caught more with my two-bob rod and sixpenny reel from Woolworths, using a bent pin as a hook.' After spending many thousands of pounds on fishing tackle over the years I would, of course, like to believe that her assertion is not entirely accurate.

Unlike my grandfather who was Abingdon born and bred, my grandmother hailed from Swindon. She moved to Abingdon at an early age to start working as a scullery maid at a large house that backed onto the Thames. Progressing to the level of cook in just a few years, she had to leave after meeting and marrying my grandfather. Together they purchased a two-up, two-down terraced house for £100 and lived there the remainder of their lives. Naturally, given her background I was never short of rock cakes, apple pies or suet puddings on my visits.

On that first day, we put our packed lunches, drinks and fishing tackle into my grandfather's creel and made the one-mile trek to the river. Being a Saturday, my grandmother would have been at work in the local grocery store located opposite the cenotaph in the centre of town. I suspect we would have called in on our way; we often did when fishing in the town.

We crossed Abingdon Town bridge, effectively moving from Berkshire to Oxfordshire (this was before the county boundary changes of 1974) and descended the steps to the river bank. A few yards upstream of the bridge the bank changed to one of grassland interspersed with cow dips that provided easy access to the water. We stopped at the first one; it was to be my fishing spot for the day.

Armed with a shrimping net attached to a cane handle, and a small bucket, both of which were undoubtedly purchased from a beach hut in Weymouth the summer before, I started paddling and fishing for fry. My grandfather sat on the higher grass bank and fished for something more substantial by casting over towards the horse chestnut trees on the opposite bank which are still furnishing children with conkers each autumn. I can recall little about the actual fishing, but I do remember the weigh-in. When it was time to leave, my bucket held over twenty small fry, whereas my grandfather had caught only one fish: a gudgeon. Although in terms of weight he had won, to a small child twenty fish beats one every time, so I considered it a success. Looking back to that first trip I do wonder the impact it may have had on me. Even now I prefer to catch more fish, rather than bigger ones. I like to see the float constantly disappearing and another fish coming to hand. Sitting for hours behind a couple of bite alarms is not my style, and it has become a running joke amongst many of my angling friends that all I catch is tiddlers. Fortunately, in matches my nets of small fish are sometimes enough to take the money.

A few years after my introduction to fishing, I had become competent with rod and reel and had taken the sport to heart. During the school holidays I was allowed to fish alone, providing I remained in sight of the bridge. This was purely for security reasons. My mother told me that if anyone, particularly adults, were causing me concern I should wave to a person on the bridge and pretend I knew them. It was a good strategy and more than adequate in those more trusting times; fortunately I never had need to execute the carefully conceived plan.

Fishing was very popular in Abingdon at the time, and it was sometimes difficult to get a peg along my preferred stretch of the Thames. I remember many occasions stopping on the bridge to look along the river and seeing every peg occupied. Given this level of interest it was not at all surprising that three different shops in the town sold fishing tackle and bait. Of these three shops my favourite was Beadles.

Located on Ock Street, Beadles was essentially the only hardware shop I looked forward to visiting. On opening the front door the sound of a bell, to alert the staff to a potential new customer, would echo above my head; looking down, the floor was concave just inside the entrance, a result of countless footsteps gradually wearing the wooden floor boards away since the shop opened in 1836; on the right a long counter ran from one end of the shop to the other, behind which stood the staff and an array of shelves that held items too numerous to count. The air was full of competing aromas: paint, timber, linseed oil, and white spirit to name but a few. It was a heady mix that promised the D-I-Y fanatic that whatever he/she needed, it could be found in Beadles, or 'Brin's' as my grandfather would refer to the shop, the name of the previous owner being Brin Gillingham.

The fishing tackle was sold at the far end of the shop. I would make my way straight there, green maggot box with a white lid in hand. For several years my request would always be the same: '10 pence worth of maggots, please'. If my grandfather was with me we would also have a close look at the floats, mostly quills, and he would inevitably buy a packet of hooks: size 10 and tied to nylon. If I did get a new float I'd use it on my next fishing outing whether it was suitable or not, the temptation to try something different was always too great. Many of these floats I still own today, but they are never used simply because I could not bear to lose any of them.

Beadles operated until 2001; according to the *Oxford Mail* at the time of its closure it was the oldest shop in Abingdon. In its place there now stand several residential flats. As is the case with many town centre shops, the competition from major retail chains and out-of-town shopping complexes, proved to be their downfall. Despite the huge population increase in Oxfordshire and around the Abingdon area, the town no longer has any outlet where anglers can buy tackle and bait, and the river is rarely fished, except for a handful of match days. Of course, anglers have a much wider choice of venues nowadays but, with safe parking nearby, it is somewhat surprising that the Thames between the lock and the Abingdon bridge is fished so infrequently.

It is fair to say that in those early days we did not catch a great deal. A couple of *goer* roach (*goers* were fish that exceed the size limits; back then it was seven inches for a roach) would have made for a good day, and a single chub over 2lbs would have been a season highlight. We did catch plenty of silver bream though, a species that I have not seen for over thirty years and one which no longer seems to inhabit the Thames in Oxfordshire. On returning home after one of these less than productive days, especially a cold day in late autumn, my grandmother would say: 'You look frozen, sit by the fire and I'll make you a cup of tea. Here's a cake.' Even without catching fish, these were good days.

With the benefit of hindsight it is easy to see why we struggled to catch. The Thames was not so prolific in those days, and our choices of bait and tackle left a lot to be desired. My grandfather targeted big fish; he used a 1950s KP Morritt Intrepid Continental reel and a bamboo/cane rod made by Milward. On purchasing the rod, the shop owner told him that it was so light he would be able to hold it all day without realising it was in his hand. As you can imagine that's not strictly true. It was also the pre-waggler era so our presentation of bait was not as good as it could have been. On some days our quill floats worked well, but at other times a waggler would have been a much better choice.

The other key reason for our less than prolific catches concerns bait. Although my grandfather had fished matches through the 1950s, and won some, we did not use groundbait, and it was several years after I started fishing that we started using maggots. His only baits were bread paste and worms. The worms, lobs and reds, would be collected from his allotment on the evening before fishing, and the paste was made on the morning of our excursions. In my mind I can still see him standing at the kitchen sink, a slice of crustless bread in his hands and the tap running. He would dampen the bread then mould it into a ball, finally wrapping it in a clean handkerchief to remove any excess water. Some days he would add any cheese left over in the larder (at this time my grandparents did not own a refrigerator or freezer). Cutting small cubes of cheddar cheese, my grandfather would add them to the ball of bread paste then continue to knead it with his hands. The cheese would soften and eventually form part of the paste. On occasions he would continue the moulding process on the bank, the result of which was a soft bread/cheese mix that was without doubt his favourite bait.

Paradoxically, I firmly believe that our relatively poor results inspired me to continue fishing. The sport became the equivalent of an unsolved puzzle. How could I catch more fish? How would I improve my chance of catching better fish? These questions needed answering. I do wonder how youngsters who get introduced to the sport at a commercial venue and catch hundreds of pounds of carp on their first few visits, view fishing. What is it that makes them return, if they do? The action of landing a decent fish is unquestionably enjoyable. But to repeat it time and time again surely takes the gloss off it. And then what? Is there a good enough reason to return? The fact we didn't catch early on definitely enticed me to continue fishing, to find better methods, to unearth better venues, and to catch more fish. Had I been successful in those early days I may not have had sufficient reason to adopt angling as my sport of choice, in which case my life would have been very different and definitely not as enjoyable.

Often, while fishing, my grandfather would claim that when he retired he would fish every day. Unfortunately that's not how events unfolded. Although he did fish more often the year after he left work, he would generally wait for the weekend when we could go together. Rapidly debilitating arthritis then prevented him from walking from the car park to the river bank, so his angling trips began to dwindle and it was clear that his lifelong dream to fish more often would never be realised. Alzheimer's disease, possibly caused by the number of times he was hit on the head while working (the council did not provide any protective clothing, not even hard hats, in those times) began to weave its cruel spell and shortly after brought the life of the man who had instilled in me the love of fishing to an untimely close.

I often think back to those early days and the weekends in Abingdon and the images that fill my mind are always the same: a roaring fire in the grate; cakes and apple pies; and fishing for roach with breadpaste or worms.

CHAPTER 11

WORMS EVERYWHERE

*Critical bait management; being careful
where you walk; angling camaraderie;
the importance of keeping the lid on a bait tub.*

Outside it is cold and dark; inside it's just cold: the central heating won't power up until 8am, which is over an hour from now. The weather forecast suggests a dry, overcast morning, in other words the perfect day for fishing and perfect weather for me. Unlike many anglers, I never fish well in the rain, it seems to cause me to get into more tangles than usual, and trying to lift fish to hand while sheltering under a large umbrella is altogether more difficult than without one. The dull skies are another meteorological bonus: a certain species of fish possesses exceptional eyesight which enables them to hunt more effectively in low light conditions when they are less likely to be spotted by the prey fish they seek. This is an evolutionary trait that has served them well for millennia. The fact that these fish will be feeding for longer is good news for the PAC Match Anglers since the stretch of the canal we have been allocated to fish today is, apparently, full of them. Today's main focus will be perch.

With my sandwiches and coffee prepared, I'm ready to go. I'm not entirely sure why, but I feel very positive about today's match. Opening the door from the kitchen to the garage I feel the even cooler air from the darkened room on my face. I press the light switch and the two fluorescent strip-lights slowly flicker to life simulating a strobe effect. As I wait for the bulbs to become fully illuminated, I catch sight of something unexpected on the garage floor. It is probably a dried, curled leaf, or errant twig from my kit; I really should sweep up more often. As the light improves I can see that my initial assessment was far from correct. To my horror, it's not a twig or a leaf, it's a worm. And it's alive.

Looking left and right, I can see worms everywhere: on the treads of a step ladder, on my workbench, clinging to the front of the washing machine, stuck to the sides of the fridge and freezer, everywhere. There's even one trying his best to get inside one of my trainers – maybe his mate is already in there. Many of the worms are not looking their best. In fact if they had legs then most of them would be on their last: the dry surfaces and dust is drying them out quickly. This is, no doubt, not how they, nor I, had planned to start the day.

Collecting as many as I can, I return them to the bait tub from which they had escaped. Judging by the number that remain, a large proportion have simply disappeared. But where? And will I, or more worryingly Sara, ever find out?

We were supposed to be meeting in the market square in Wantage at 7:15am, that was fifteen minutes ago so I am not surprised to find it empty. As I leave the former Roman settlement, birthplace of King Alfred (the only Monarch given the title 'Great') and legendary racehorse jockey Lester Piggott, and head southwards, my journey takes me over the Ridgeway, then across the desolate, wind-swept North Berkshire Downs, before I descend to a lower plain carved out over many thousands of years by the rivers Dun and Kennet. I am now in a rather deserted-looking Hungerford. Had this been the second Tuesday after Easter then the streets would be filled with revellers celebrating the English medieval festival of *Hocktide*; fortunately today is a Sunday in early February.

Finally the car park of Hungerford's medical centre, our allotted parking area for the day, is within view. I know I am late, very late, but I do have an excuse. Much to my amazement the Match Secretary doesn't even mention it. With my gear on the barrow I tag onto the end of a long snaking line of anglers making their way to the canal. Today we are fishing the Church Stretch and for newcomers like me there's no prize for guessing why it is so named. As we walk through the churchyard, a clamour of rooks attempt to serenade us. Their harsh, abrasive calls are hardly a match for the harmonious tones that constitute the dawn chorus in the Spring, and are more likely to inspire images of the opening scenes of so many Hammer horror films. In fact I would not be too surprised to see Christopher Lee pass by in a carriage pulled by a pair of black horses at any moment. A dog walker interrupts these rather random thoughts.

'What are you pushing?' she asks.

'Fishing tackle.'

'Do you really need all that?'

It's a good point, we do seem to take more and more tackle each year. This is a direct result of fishing in matches. Often, after a match I'll be certain that with a different rig, pole elastic or bait, I could have caught many more fish. Consequently, I buy more tackle and bait ready for the next contest. After a few years, this begins to mount up. Soon a larger seatbox or rod bag or barrow is required, even though a great deal of the new tackle will only have been used occasionally in very niche circumstances. This is not a new phenomenon though.

In *Coburn's Kalendar of Amusements in Town and Country for 1840*, it is recommended that a wide range of rods are kept for different types of fishing. For legering, a rod of no less than 15ft ideally made from 'white East India cane' is suggested. Punt fishing, it is claimed, requires a much smaller rod of around 12ft with a bamboo construction preferred. Unlike today's short lure rods, the author proposes a 14ft rod made from a sturdy wood such as greenheart for spinning for jack pike. Greenheart is again the choice for salmon rods, although hickory is also mentioned. These rods need to be at least 16ft long with some exceeding 21ft. Although the shorter rods would have been easier to handle, they would still weigh around 2lbs 8oz each. The float rod I use, purchased around 150 years later, weighs a mere 6.35oz (180g).

The type of material used for the handle was hotly debated. Some anglers opted for the heavier ash handles that should be 'of the finest and longest grain, highly seasoned, cut from the inside of an old, straight, and ungnarled tree'. The alternative was willow, a much lighter wood. However, it was claimed that willow had less elasticity than ash and in general a greater number of knots. One proponent for ash asserted quite acerbically that 'for a person of rather feeble arm, and not inclined to hard work, the willow-butt will be better.' Most surprisingly, the *The Secrets of Angling* published in 1885 details how the top sections of these rods should be coloured, stating that white or grey 'offend the least'. Ghost tops for poles are clearly not a twentieth century invention.

I've joined the main group of anglers awaiting the draw and can see many of the usual members, plus one I have not fished a match with for several months. Andy is tall, in fact he's head and shoulders above many of us and not just in height: he is also a brilliant angler. I nod, and he smiles by return.

'Phil told me about your parking incident at the river,' he says smiling.

'Yeah, I know, we almost got that very badly wrong.'

He laughs. Andy tends to fish a handful of matches each year, and he wins many of them. He is more of a big fish angler so in the summer he is after carp, in the winter he targets big perch and pike. That's when he is in the UK. Andy lives for his fishing and his love of the sport means he is often in some very unusual places. The results of his globe-trotting are nothing short of amazing. From Kazakhstan to Guyana, from USA to Thailand via most mainland European countries, Andy has landed fish that even the *Monster Carp* presenters would envy. In Egypt he caught a 161lbs Nile Perch; in Surinam a 200lbs paraiba catfish. A sturgeon estimated to be 500lbs in the USA supplemented a 153lbs alligator gar on a particularly memorable trip; and in Guyana he was fortunate to land a 230lbs arapaima. Of all the wonderful fish he has caught, Andy rates the Mekong Catfish as the hardest fighting fish he has so far encountered, while lure fishing for peacock bass accounted for some of the most enjoyable excursions. Today he will be fishing for far less exotic fish: perch of up to 2lbs; roach of mostly less than 6oz; skimmer bream; and the hard-fighting gudgeon that will probably not exceed 2oz. There will be no need for his 200lbs braided mainline today.

The draw is progressing well, and apparently only three pegs remain: the two end pegs and peg 5. I'm next to draw, finally I will get an end peg. Well, there's a two in three chance I will and that's good enough odds for me. Why is the end peg so important? A quick check of the results answers that query. In all canal matches, the end pegs have accounted for half of all wins. That's how important getting an end peg is.

'Pete, you get, hang on they're in there somewhere,' Danny is rummaging around in the drawstring bag trying to grab one of the three remaining tokens. 'Got one, you're on peg 5.'

To say I am deflated is an understatement. On the plus side Andy did not get an end peg, those two most coveted pegs were shared between Danny (again) and Nick. A graph of my chance of winning as the draw progressed would have been steadily rising followed by a cliff-edge type fall. There's nothing I can do about it except complain, so that's what I do, good-humouredly though. I also try a little psychology by reminding Danny that he should win easily from the downstream end peg.

Peg 5 is situated directly behind the church; not that that is an issue, of far more importance is the fact that I have Leslie to my left and Bill on peg 4 to my right. Being sandwiched between two top class canal anglers is not great with respect to my chance of success, but it provides an opportunity to learn from experts. One positive is that I'd much rather be here than on peg 6: Leslie's peg is located in the mouth of the lock; he has no cover on the far bank, and apparently no features at all to fish to. He's in for a tough day. Bill is not without his issues either. Directly behind his peg lies a pile of mess that only the very largest of dogs could have deposited. Despite its enormous size he has already managed to disturb it – twice. Each occasion was accompanied by an outburst of language not entirely in harmony with the hallowed surroundings. He is now suffering the consequences of the smell. Luckily, the slight downstream wind is protecting me, but it has already put Bill off his early morning piece of cake.

Dog mess is not the only hazard faced by canal towpath users. As well as looking at what they might be about to step in, it's just as necessary to keep an eye open for cyclists. The vast majority of bikers take great care when cycling past a group of anglers or walkers, slowing and occasionally stopping. There are, inevitably, a few that speed along the towpath as if they were in a time trial for Olympic selection and refusing to decelerate for anything or anyone. Families with young children are at most danger. It does seem to be an inconsistency that cyclists are not permitted to ride on pavements, yet they are allowed to speed along towpaths which are, in places, even narrower. Given the combination of groups of people, loose dogs, an uneven surface, and speeding bicycles, it is surprising that there are not even more accidents.

When there is an angling-related incident in a match it often involves Bill and the number six section of his pole. In fact, for this particular combination of angler and item of fishing tackle, when troubles come they come not as single spies, to borrow a phrase from a sixteenth century playwright from Stratford. Not so long ago, on a different stretch of the canal, a free-roaming Labrador managed to divide the pole section into two much shorter lengths. Fortunately Bill, a top class angler and much-liked by everyone in the club, was able to replace it in time for the next match for the princely sum of £130. But he really should not have bothered. Roughly two hours into this event, with his shiny new section fresh from the protective bubble wrap and in use for the very first time, a sprightly octogenarian who was enjoying a relaxing Sunday morning walk along the canal decided to test her agility. Rather than waiting for Bill to move the delicate item of carbon fibre that was positioned on his pole rollers (at least two feet off the ground) and blocking the towpath, she attempted to climb over it. While initially all was progressing smoothly, a sudden, loud crack suggested the confidence the walker held in her climbing ability had been misplaced. A sincere apology followed, but taken by complete surprise, and in a certain amount of shock, the septuagenarian angler's reply comprised a rather injudicious phrase: 'At your age,' he started 'why are you trying to get your leg over?'

Another £130 was soon on its way to a tackle supplier, and as many of the club members remarked, 'Bill, at least you know where to get a spare from.' Unsurprisingly, he was not the slightest bit amused.

Add to those breakages the time he dropped the jinxed section into the Thames and there's the basis for a comedy to rival Laurel and Hardy. This particular calamity required the use of a borrowed ladder to enable Bill to descend from the top of the high, vertical bank to the water's edge in order to retrieve his most troublesome item of fishing tackle. In the process, several Thames Path walkers were treated to the sight of a then 71-year-old man emerging from the river in just a pair of wet underpants. I was fully expecting a local TV news team to appear shortly after, keen to cover a shocking new craze sweeping through Oxfordshire: naked OAP wild swimmers.

Despite these mishaps, and many others including once being pushed into the river by his own dog, Bill's biggest complaint, one he reiterates time and time again, is that he never draws an end peg. He's already mentioned that to me at least three times this morning!

We are just over thirty minutes into the match: Bill has had a skimmer, some roach, and is now landing a large plastic carrier bag; I've had a few roach; Leslie has yet to get a bite. Today I have opted for a slightly different baiting approach. There's a pronounced shelf near to the far bank directly in front of me. While this is not unusual for a canal, in other stretches it has been eroded to a gentle slope from about three quarters of the way across to the far bank. Here it is a dramatic change of depth possibly due to a different substrate. Rather than feeding worms down the track I have potted some to this ledge, and have only fed groundbait in the deeper water where I will also loose feed and fish with maggots or pinkies.

It must be 10am because the church bell has just sounded its call to the local parishioners. In fact the churchgoers would not need to be local to hear it, such is the volume. Does anyone have any ear plugs?

Almost two hours in and I've matched Bill's skimmer with one of my own of a similar size. I have also been fortunate with my groundbait line producing several small roach. Bill's catch rate has slowed and Leslie still awaits his first bite of the day. I confidently expect the end pegs to be fishing well though. Interestingly there have been very few boats today, not that they are a great problem. Most just cruise by, keeping as far away from the anglers' lines as possible with the boaters exchanging a few light-hearted comments with those of us on the bank. Canal boats never seem to be in a rush to get anywhere. Unfortunately the same cannot be said for many of the boats that speed along the Thames.

Just past halfway and my groundbait line has slowed but I have had a perch from the far bank. Leslie is now off the mark; he has had one bite which produced a 4oz perch. To have a chance he will need to produce a remarkable second half though. Bill is still picking off a few fish, but I suspect I am just in front of him. Apparently Nick and Danny are catching – that's something I don't want to hear.

Into the last hour now and the perch line has picked up well. I'm catching a fish every drift and although they are mostly small, some have been over 8oz and one would be just over a pound. There's a problem though: I am running out of worms, in fact I've only two left. I can only assume there are more hiding in the garage than I had at first thought.

'You got those perch lined up over there?' Bill asks.

'There are plenty there, would you like me ask some of them to swim down to you?'

'If you don't mind.'

'Problem is I've run out of worms,' I add.

'I've got some you can have,' Leslie interjects.

'Really?'

'Yes, have them all, I can't get a bite.'

Even though we are fishing against each other, Leslie is more than happy for me to take his bait and in the process reduce his chance of winning and improve mine. This outstanding offer of generosity is like a footballer giving his opposite number his boots and electing to play in socks. There are few sports where such a degree of magnanimity would be found.

With my newly-acquired bait I kept catching perch until the final whistle. I think I have done well, but that probably means the end pegs have done much better. The weigh-in could be a tense affair.

Danny has decided that the weigh-in will start with Nick on peg 12. This means he thinks he has a chance of winning and wants to leave his net until last. It certainly has the effect of increasing the tension. Nick weighs in 5lbs 4oz, a good weight, and I am not entirely sure I have beaten him. The remaining anglers upstream of the lock have not fared well; even Andy only weighed in 1lb 15oz. Yet again the end peg has proved how valuable it is.

Downstream of the lock, Leslie weighed in one perch for 4oz. Now it's my turn. The net feels much heavier than I expected, so I am sure I have more than 5lbs.

'You can't weigh that in,' Bill exclaims pointing to the end of the net. Looking more closely I can see a large branch tangled in the mesh, no wonder the net felt so heavy. With the extraneous detritus removed, and the 54 fish on the scales I can see the dial moving past 5lbs. So I'll be in the lead, at least for a short while.

'Six six,' Danny says in a slightly exasperated fashion. Maybe he's not done as well as I thought, I'm pleased with 6lbs 6oz though.

'You'll beat that won't you Danny?' asks Gary.

'No, I've got hardly anything.'

'Well, you've got at least one perch pushing two pounds, I saw you net it just before the whistle,' Gary continues.

'It's not two pounds,' he moans, 'barely a pound I reckon.' None of us believes him.

Gary's comment is of concern; a two-pounder supplemented with roach and small perch would be enough to beat me. Gary weighs in 3lbs, and no one else downstream of me has matched my weight. It just depends on what Danny has in his net.

There's a deal of splashing as Danny gently lifts his net in, which is not a sound that fills me with confidence. With the fish in the weigh sling it looks like his weight will be similar to mine. The big perch is not 2lbs, more like a pound and a half, that's in my favour, but he has a lot of small roach.

I'm holding the scales and Gary is reading them.

'Come on Gary this is making my arms ache.'

'The needle keeps bouncing around, keep the fish still.' A few more agonising seconds go by. 'Danny, you've got, let me see, five pounds one ounce.'

So it wasn't as close as I thought and I managed to get the verdict with the two end pegs taking second and third. The worms that Leslie gave me certainly made the difference: without them I probably would not have won. When the primary aim of the day's sport is to enjoy it, such good spirit among match anglers is priceless. Fortunately good spirit is not something the PAC match anglers lack.

A few days after the canal match, Sara needed to get something from the local shop. It was raining so I suggested she took the umbrella. No sooner had she left, she was back. Concerned at her speedy return, I went outside to see what the problem was. Sara merely beckoned me under the brolly.

Pointing towards the underside of the umbrella, she said 'What's that?'

Hanging full length from one of the stays right in front of her eyes was a dendrobaena worm.

'Oh, I could have done with that on Sunday,' I said by way of a reply and an attempt to lighten the atmosphere.

'Just get rid of it,' came the terse response.

I returned the worm to the bait tub, marvelling at how resourceful they are. Without the benefit of sight, it is amazing where they end up. To get inside an umbrella was an achievement well beyond the expectations of such a creature, and perfectly illustrates their levels of determination and tenacity. That was my view, later it was made very clear that Sara held a different opinion.

A worm trapped inside an umbrella, though unusual, is far from the worst bait-related mishap I have encountered over the years. I remember, as a child, dropping a whole tub of maggots in my bedroom – why they were in there I have no idea. What I can clearly remember is the speed at which they can burrow into the fibres of a carpet, and how difficult and time-consuming it is, using a pin, to extricate them one at a time whilst crawling around the floor. Unlike many people who learn from such experiences, as I have grown older I seem to forget the lessons of these historical events. Rather than shaping my behaviour for the better, they simply drift quietly into the mists of time never to have any significant impact on my future actions.

Until just a few years ago I used to keep my maggots, pinkies and worms in the refrigerator in the kitchen. I know what you are thinking, but they were all in sealed boxes with no possibility of escape. Or so I believed. One Monday morning when Sara was preparing breakfast, and I was still dozing, I heard her call my name. Maybe, as a special treat,

Sara had cooked a full English breakfast. Is there a better way to start the day? I raced downstairs fully convinced that I would soon be enjoying all the delights fried food could offer. As I neared the kitchen I began to get slightly concerned, there was no smell of crispy bacon, or even of toast. 'Just one egg for me,' I called out making my way through the living room, more in hope than expectation. By way of a reply, there was sullen silence. As I entered the kitchen Sara simply pointed and said 'There are worms all over the fridge.'

'So, there's no fry-up then?'

Claiming there were worms 'all over the fridge' was a slight exaggeration. Worms were indeed on the loose in the fridge, but hardly all over it. Apparently, when Sara had grabbed a pot of yoghurt she felt something damp. At first she thought the pot had leaked, but after turning it could see a good-sized dendrobaena adhered to the plastic. A subsequent closer inspection revealed the scale of the problem and prompted her to call me.

Naturally, while Sara was at work that day I set about cleaning the fridge and returning the rogue worms to the tub which I found was not properly closed. I never leave the lid partially open on my bait tubs, so this was something that called for more investigation.

By the evening, I had solved the mystery and decided to reveal my findings to Sara as she returned from work.

'This is how the worms got out,' I proudly announced. 'Remember when I got back from the match? You were doing something in the fridge and I gave you the two tubs of maggots and pinkies to put away, then the worms.' Surprisingly there was not a flicker of agreement on Sara's face, so I continued. 'Well, when you put the worms in, next to the maggots, the lip of the lid of the worm box rubbed along the lid of the maggot tub and in so doing it was raised up a little. Worms can get through even the smallest of gaps, so that's how they escaped,' I ended with a smile, a flourish if you will, but all I got back was a cold, hard stare. Maybe a round of applause would have been too much to ask, but I was at least anticipating a certain amount of congratulations on my Sherlock Holmes-like deductive reasoning and the detailed explanation I was able to provide. So I carried on which, given the benefit of hindsight, was a mistake: 'So it actually wasn't me who caused the worms to escape, because I didn't...' at this point the stare had become a definite scowl. I considered my options and concluded that it was probably best if I let Sara have time to absorb the implications of my findings. Quite remarkably, Sara said nothing about the incident all evening, in fact she said nothing at all. Nor the next morning.

Like the adverts that state a particular Christmas gift can give 'hours of fun for all the family' escaped worms can provide 'days of frustration for all the family'. A few days after the escaped worms episode, Sara complained that there was an awful smell in the fridge suggesting that my bait was the cause. After some careful checking, I was certain that the strawberries were the source of the problem, and convinced Sara that this was the case. Strawberries can smell quite badly when kept in a fridge.

The day after, Sara again complained about the fridge but, this time, there were no strawberries to blame. I assured her that I had thoroughly cleaned the fridge, and that the bait did not smell. This time she was not convinced. Fortunately that same day I was fishing at a local lake and mentioned the odorous fridge to an angling friend. 'Have you checked the water tray?' he asked. I didn't even know such a thing existed, so back at home I removed the tray which is intended to catch condensation and other spillages. In it there was a small amount of water mixed with some type of dairy product, possibly milk or cream. But to my horror, amongst this thick, unedifying gloop lay three or four dead worms. After escaping from the bait tub they that had managed to wriggle through the drain outlet. The smell was horrendous; maggots can smell bad, but dead worms are off the scale.

On Sara's return from work I told her that the rather off-putting fridge aroma had been eliminated and replaced by one more fitting a clean kitchen appliance. I was about to explain how I had solved yet another problem, and show that it was related to the earlier worm issue for which I was not to blame, but quickly thought better of it. After all our cake supply was running low and I really enjoy a homemade Victoria Sandwich.

Not long after this somewhat tortuous bait episode, Gordon, a good friend and PAC member, was able to get me a small bait fridge that I now keep in the garage. It is something I recommend that all anglers acquire, that's if they want to retain a reasonable degree of harmony at home.

CHAPTER 12

CLOSING DAY

Last chance; chub fishing;
giving the sport a future.

It's 7am. Usually at this time on a weekday I am safely tucked up in a nice warm bed, as having read the earlier chapters you are well aware. Today, though, I am perched on the banks of the river Thames, in the same peg I fished on the opening day back in June. The outlook is very different as it always is when the season draws to a close. There's little greenery in front of me, the willow trees having been reduced to stumps, and the reeds are no longer resplendent in their various shades of emerald. The river holds much more water than last June, but at least it is fishable; so many final days have been ruined by floods in recent years. I'm not sure that has improved my chances of catching though, the Thames can be tricky at this time of the year. I opted to leave the pole at home today and will just fish the feeder rod. My hope is that somewhere, not far from where I cast my line, lies a huge chub. Even better would be a huge hungry chub. Taking the Match Secretary's advice, after all he has dedicated far more time to catching chub than I have, I am fishing with cheesepaste. He also told me to have patience. The cheesepaste I can manage, not so sure about the patience.

It's 8am, the rod tip has remained stubbornly still, my flask is half empty and I only have two sandwiches left. Fishing the feeder means I no longer have to repeatedly reposition a float or lift it so that the bait moves temptingly through the watercourse. Without these diversions to occupy me, I eat and drink. Instead, I should focus more on the water, learn what I can, then make changes to improve the chance that I catch my intended fish. While I did try that earlier, there's little to see; the river rumbles by, there are no fish topping, and no other anglers to copy. So it is quickly back to the sandwiches and coffee. Maybe I should try a different peg, or different bait? Izaak Walton recommended using worms for chub in March, unfortunately I didn't bring any, trusting Danny's advice implicitly. That is beginning to look like an error of judgement. At least, according to Walton, I am fishing where the chub are most likely to be. In cold weather Izaak recommended fishing on the river bed. At warmer times of year his advice was to search the upper layers of the water, with a grasshopper the perfect bait.

Writing in the *Kalendar of Amusement (1840)*, the fishing correspondent recommended *dibbing* for chub. This approach is essentially free-lining with a rod and a large insect for bait and has similarities to modern day *dobbing* for carp. The angler first needs to identify a place where the chub may be, and allow the bait to drop quietly onto the water. Then for the *dibbing*. According to the correspondent, 'by repeatedly tapping the butt-end of the rod, the bait is moved in a manner resembling the struggles of a living insect, and he is sure to take the largest fish in the hole.' Without a large insect for bait, or a likely looking chub-holding spot within a rod length's distance, I cannot put this theory to the test though I am sure it would work under the right conditions. Today, I just need to have more patience and I am sure one of these 'fearfullest of fishes' will be along soon.

So why do I, and millions like me, turn up on days when their time would be better spent doing something totally different, often in weather that is more conducive to sitting in front of the television, and at times when they know that success is unlikely? Well, the simple answer is: fishing is addictive; I've always fished and cannot think of a time when I won't fish. There are days when anglers just have to go fishing. Apparently, running has the same effect. I cannot see how anyone can enjoy running, yet there are people who run two or three times each week. They get something from it which others simply cannot appreciate. The same applies to fishing: anglers get a huge amount of pleasure from attempting to catch fish and once the angling drug gets into your veins, it becomes impossible to dispel.

This wonderful allure that fishing possesses does not just take over the lives of a specific sector of society. It's a sport for everyone which is why it has appealed to so many for so long. Writing in *Bailey's Sports and Pastimes (1893)*, the correspondent concluded *'For the hard-worked city, or worn-out professional man, the surroundings of such a day's*

*outing on the River Thames are pleasant indeed. One has
perfect quiet, fresh air, freedom from labour, rest for the brain,
and can choose agreeable companions.'*

Few, if any, sports can offer more.

Mike Brearley asserted 'above all, we are fascinated by
the complexity and variety of the game' when writing about
cricket. This also applies to fishing; I am not sure that running
can be characterised in the same way, its addictive qualities
must be rooted in some other facet of the exercise. Angling
can be complex, a quick read through the *Angling Times* will
confirm that. But one of its many appealing factors is that it
also can be very straightforward. For those not particularly
interested in catching more than others, the simplest of tackle,
bait, and method can produce the desired results. At the other
end of the scale, the commercial match anglers have taken the
sport to a much higher level. In a single match, competitors
can use a vast array of methods, as well as a multitude of baits
to improve their weight of fish.

Naturally, a sport that offers potential participants a
range of different approaches will attract more people. This is
where angling holds a major advantage over all other sports.
From sea fishing by boat, from piers, and off beaches, to trout
fishing in lakes and rivers, and coarse fishing with its plethora
of disciplines, there's something to suit every personality. For
those who are prepared to wait, sometimes days, for a bite,
then targeting specimen fish would be first choice. The less
patient among us, who would prefer to see the float going
under every few seconds, are better suited to fishing for a
smaller quarry. And for the angler who prefers to carry a
small amount of kit, and keep on the move, then lure fishing
is surely the ideal way to spend a day by the bank. In its many
guises, fishing has much to offer.

It's 9am: there's one sandwich and roughly one cup of coffee left. Needless to say there's been no activity on the fishing front. The mallards that provided so much entertainment back in the summer have returned, although their number has been reduced from three to two. Maybe the resident otter fancied a change for his Christmas meal and opted for duck rather than fish. I've decided to persevere for another hour, maybe an hour and a half, then accept grudgingly the season is over.

Not many years ago, fishing was by far the most popular participant sport in Great Britain. This is no longer the case, apparently, with football now heading the list. However, this assessment largely depends on which data set is to be believed. What we do know about fishing is that the number of individuals who fish during the year is in the millions. Yet even at over a million, large swathes of the population do not fish, and many reasons have been given for this by those attempting to attract more anglers onto the banks of the lakes, canals and rivers. The main cause is that many people do not have a family tradition of fishing. In my experience, most anglers were introduced to the sport by parents or grandparents. Without this support and encouragement they would not have become anglers.

Some sections of the UK population simply do not have that tradition and as a result fishing is not even considered to be an option for their leisure time. This is not quite so important in other sports. Neither Sara nor I have ever been interested in trampolining, yet our daughter became quite accomplished at the sport. The reason for this was a very simple one: each week we were able to take her to a trampolining lesson, leave her for an hour or two, enjoy the relatively cheap childcare, then return to collect her.

Similar coaching facilities are available for most sports, but not fishing. In mid-Devon there's a venue which allows people to hire a rod and fish for an hour for a fixed fee. It's not all that's on offer, there's a café, restaurant, and other attractions, and given it's location it is of course aimed at families enjoying their summer holidays.

There's no reason why the larger commercial angling centres could not set up similar facilities. A small pond could be added to the complex, and an instructor/coach could be engaged to provide lessons to those interested in the sport. With on-site cafes, there would be places for parents, if they chose not to take part, to wait for their children. The lake's owners would make money from the café purchases, and from the person running the programme, while the instructor would profit directly from those attending. If those taking part in the activity decided to take an even greater interest in fishing, I have no doubt that the on-site tackle shop could provide the necessary equipment. Naturally this would take investment, but it might be money well spent.

Such an initiative would benefit from the Environment Agency introducing a 'Lake Licence' to cover the venue, which would ease the unnecessary bureaucracy for any prospective anglers, making it a more attractive option. As a sport, fishing is very much in the minority when it comes to a requirement for national licensing. Allowing the owner to cover a lake for educational purposes seems an obvious move in the quest to attract more people into the sport.

It's 10am. About five minutes ago I had what I thought was a small indication on the rod tip. It may have been a crayfish, or a piece of debris catching the line as it drifts downstream. But of course it may also have been a chub taking a cursory interest in my cheesepaste. I'll wait a little longer, just to check.

Unlike many sports, anyone can fish. Anglers do not need to be exceptionally fit, tall, slim, or of a specific age to gain pleasure from the sport. I have fished against men and women, experts and novices, adults and juniors, the able-bodied and less able-bodied including a man with one arm, and on many occasions they have caught more than me. For those with a competitive streak, they do not need to have attended specialist coaching sessions, and while sponsorship deals help with funding the costs of travel and bait, with hard work and dedication any angler can make it into the elite class. There are no barriers in fishing, no discrimination, and no glass ceilings.

It's 10:45am and finally I have a fish on. It may not be the huge chub I was hoping for but it is at least a chub. The fish is in the net now and I can see that it is no more than a pound. In his book Izaak Walton targeted and caught the largest chub from a shoal of twenty fish, I've ended up with the smallest. Oh well, it's always nice to end the season with a fish.

Loading my kit into the car, I pause to look back at the river one last time. While watching the water making its way unrelentingly under the ancient bridge to the towns and cities beyond, my thoughts wander back in time. Throughout my life, so much of which has already slipped through my hands in what seems like hardly any time at all, I've made many decisions, many thousands in fact (mostly related to horseracing, but that's another story). Two of the more significant that come immediately to mind were to marry Sara (fortunately she agreed with that one) and to adopt fishing as my main pastime.

Sara has been the key to any modest successes I have had. Without her support, advice and guidance, I would not have been able to follow such an unusual, and rewarding path through life. My family have also played an important role, especially our daughter Rhianna who somehow always manages to keep me grounded with a perceptive observation or question such as: 'Dad, how come Danny caught 20lbs of fish in the match and you only caught 4lbs from the next peg?' Fishing also has had a role and has become the equivalent to a dependable, uncritical silent partner in a business arrangement. It's always there when a distraction is needed, never passes judgement on any mistakes that may have been made, and provides endless entertainment. In both respects I could not have chosen better.

I freely admit that I have been very lucky in life (my match colleagues would say that certainly applies to fishing) which has gently glided along, only occasionally encountering an eddy that caused a ripple of disturbance or slight change of course. Given the chance to repeat the last forty years, the only change I would make is to start match fishing sooner. Match fishing invokes its particular type of camaraderie.

Although we are competing against each other, we still want everyone to catch well. Winning a match with a good weight at a venue that has fished well is somehow more satisfying than winning with just a few ounces of fish in the net on a hard day. Amongst the match anglers at the PAC, some are far more competitive than others and would do anything within the rules to win; others just enjoy a day that promises a relaxing few hours fishing, a chance to catch up with friends, and the possibility of a payout at the end. Like the sport itself, match fishing has something to offer every angler. Admittedly, the early morning starts are difficult to get used to; and the longer drives, especially in the winter, are far from welcome, but overall there is plenty to gain from taking part.

After a match, with heads full of thoughts and ideas for future fishing trips, we go home where hopefully we will find a nice cup of tea waiting. Once settled in the comfort of the house, cup in one hand, piece of cake in the other, we can regale whoever may be lucky enough to be within earshot, wife, child, or pet, with the story of the match: what went right; what went wrong; why we didn't catch more; who got lucky; what we'd change next time; why we didn't win; and most importantly how we would have won if only we had drawn an end peg.

REFERENCES

Bailey, J., *50 Fish to Catch Before You Die*

Cholmondeley-Pennel, H., *Fishing*

Dickens' C., *Dickens' Dictionary of the Thames*

Hall, S.C. and Hall, A.M., *The book of the Thames from its rise to its fall*

Harvey, B., *Living and Dying in England 1100-1540 : The Monastic Experience*

Jackson, G. F., *Shropshire Folk-Lore: A Sheaf of Gleanings (C.S. Burne Ed.)*

'JD', *The Secrets of Angling*

Jess, E., *An Angler's Rambles*

Lloyd, L., *Scandinavian Adventures.*

Opie, I., Tatem, M. (eds.), *A Dictionary of Superstitions*

Reeves, B (Ed.), *Colburn's Kalendar of Amusements in Town and Country for 1840*

'RH', *Angling Improved*

Scott, K., *Mammoths and Neanderthals in the Thames Valley*

Senior, W., *Roach-Fishing As A Fine Art in Fishing* by H.Cholmondeley-Pennel

Venables, R., *The Experienced Angler*

Walton, I., *The Compleat Angler*

Periodicals

Angling Times

Bailey's Magazine of Sports and Pastimes, various volumes

Harpers Weekly

The Fishing Gazette

Selected Websites

www.canalrivertrust.org.uk

www.gov.uk/freshwater-rod-fishing-rules/fish-size-and-catch-limits

www.thames.me.uk

https://www.adrianflux.co.uk/victorian-homes/unusual-victorian-food/

http://the-east-end.co.uk/tubby-isaac/